Yo, Blacken This!

HELL'S KITCHEN MEETS THE FRENCH QUARTER AT THE DELTA GRILL

Yo, Blacken This!

HELL'S KITCHEN MEETS THE FRENCH QUARTER AT THE DELTA GRILL

INTRODUCTION BY STEVE DANEY

TEXT BY M.B. ROBERTS • PHOTOGRAPHY BY RONALD C. MODRA

WILLOW CREEK PRESS
Minocqua, Wisconsin

© 1999 Willow Creek Press

Published by Willow Creek Press
P.O. Box 147 • Minocqua, Wisconsin 54548

Design: Heather M. McElwain

For information on other Willow Creek titles, call 1-800-850-9453.

Library of Congress Cataloging-in-Publication Data

Roberts, M.B. (Mary Beth)

Yo, blacken this! : Hell's Kitchen meets the French Quarter at the Delta Grill / introduction by Steve Daney ; text by M.B. Roberts ; photography by Ronald C. Modra.

    p.   cm.

   ISBN 1-57223-280-3

   1. Cookery, Cajun. 2. Cookery, American-- Louisiana style. I. Title.

TX715.2.L68R63   1999

641.59763--dc21   99-40955

                        CIP

Printed in Canada

CHEF'S NOTE

This book is made up of my favorite Cajun recipes, many which were inspired during the years I trained with Chef Paul Prudhomme at K. Paul's in New Orleans. Since most of these dishes are served at New York City's Delta Grill, they have been adapted and updated for the most demanding of restaurant-goers, New Yorkers. I love em. I call these dishes Cajun — with New York attitude.

A note to readers: In the recipes, I switch back and forth between margarine and butter, peanut oil and olive oil, etc. My choices are intentional (for example, margarine works best when caramelizing vegetables) but are not meant to be the law. In most instances, substitutions are fine! No recipe is meant to be followed to the letter — all great cooks improvise either out of necessity or for fun. When I say *a 10" skillet*, that would probably work best. But if you use an 8" skillet, what? I'm gonna come to your house?

In other cases, I don't specify. That means your choice! For example, "milk" means whole, 2% or skim.

Also, using hats, I've rated the recipes for difficulty:

1 = easiest, 4 = most difficult.

Not for nothing cooking is supposed to be fun, relaxing, sensuous and wonderful. So, you be the chef. Have a ball.

                                — Chef Greg Tatis

TABLE OF CONTENTS

DEDICATION FROM CHEF GREG TATIS

In dedicating this book, I would like to make a testament to one of the greatest chefs of all time.

He is the only American chef ever to be awarded the coveted *Merite Agricole*. He has published five incredibly successful and beloved cook-books. He has traveled the world to share his knowledge at shows and schools.

To me, this man is the ambassador of quality, for food and for life. Of course I am speaking about Paul Prudhomme. I hope I've done him proud with this book.

Love, Greg

ACKNOWLEDGMENTS FROM THE TWO TOMS

Our heartfelt thanks to Daniel Antonelli, Jim Gilmartin, Howie Singer, Bob Jones, Joan Gallo, and the resident Superstar, Paul Gordon.

Thanks also to: Rich Barker, Bill Brink, John McKinley, Michael Volkoff, Gene Mahoney, Michael Kay, Steve Daney, Tom McCallen and Carl Mazzella.

From Tom Sullivan:
Thanks to Shane, Leroy, and my friends and family, especially my parents, Kate and Jim.

From Tom Burns:
To my parents, Joseph and Patricia Burns, thanks for putting up with me.
To Andrew Hotte, thanks to the best pool-shooting delivery boy on the west side.
To Myra, thanks for all your support over the years--but you still can't use the cash register.
And thanks to "Louisiana Lightning," Ron Guidry, a Cajun Yankee and my favorite all-time baseball player.

INTRODUCTION

New York City is an awesome town for food. Walk down the street and you're bombarded by choices . . . Italian food, Chinese food, Indian food. Not only are the choices there, but chances are you'll find the best place to have whatever kind of food you're craving. Just by asking around.

That's what happened when I visited NYC back in 1998. I was in town for a few days and wanted to stop by as many great restaurants as I could. I was in a bar near my hotel sipping a martini when the bartender, J.G., and I got to talking about New Orleans, where I live and work as chef to the mayor.

"You want great Cajun food?" he said. "Go to the Delta Grill."

Even though I was having withdrawals for some of my hometown food, I wasn't that jazzed about going. I'd never heard of a good New York Cajun place. Plus, every time I'd try "a great Cajun place" anywhere outside of New Orleans recommended by the locals, I'd always end up disappointed. But, I decided to humor J.G. and stop by The Delta Grill on my way to Le Cirque or The Rainbow Room. Hey, the guy made a great martini.

When I got there, I immediately felt like I was in the French Quarter. The atmosphere in the place was comfortable and unpretentious. The owners, Tom Burns and Tom Sullivan, were so welcoming. Chef Greg Tatis came out and introduced himself, then went back to his kitchen and began sending out samples of everything.

The crab cakes were really delicious and I couldn't believe they had Oyster Po' Boys on the menu! I've never seen that outside of New Orleans. By the way, I never made it to Le Cirque that night. Now I recommend the Delta Grill to everyone I meet who lives in New York or who might be visiting there. And I'm in the Delta Grill every time I get into Manhattan. Last trip I ate there two nights in a row. A guy's got to have a place to get his Monday Red Beans and Rice.

The chef behind the recipes in this cookbook, Greg Tatis, is not a Louisiana boy. But he really gets it. Here's a New Yorker who worked in New Orleans for a while, got the taste and feel of Cajun food, the only original American cuisine, and brought it back to New York. He didn't forget what he learned. It's the best stuff you can get — outside of New Orleans.

The timing of this cookbook is great. Mainstream America's interest in Cajun food is booming and formerly exotic or regional ingredients, such as crawfish, are available almost everywhere now. That said though, I really like Greg's attitude about being flexible and creative — if you've got great trout in your town, go ahead and use that in the recipe, even if Louisianans would use crawfish.

Cook like a Cajun, but with New York street smarts. Enjoy.

— STEVE DANEY
Chef to Mayor Marc Morial
New Orleans, Louisiana

YO! BLACKEN THIS!

Metallic strands of blue and green Mardi Gras beads still hang from the corners of picture frames and around the necks of dark bottles of rum. Teal and red satin masks with black lace trim, the kind kept in place with a rubberband, are still strewn about behind the bar. Tiny sparkling strands of lights are still strung between hanging lamps. Mardi Gras, the third celebrated at The Delta Grill, has been over for a week. But the decorations remain, along with great anticipation.

The kitchen is abuzz. Peppers have been chopped. Crab cakes are ready for crust. Chef Greg Tatis bounds into the kitchen, taking a giant step towards the stove. He lifts the lid over his head, like a cymbal he's about to crash. He leans down and smells the simmering gumbo. He spoons himself a taste and slurps it up. "O.K.," he says, exhaling deeply.

The bartender dumps another bucket of cubes into his already bulging ice bin and fidgets with the margarita machine. He fills bowls of fresh chips and salsa and places them along the bar. Tom Burns and Tom Sullivan, (a.k.a. the two Toms — the Delta Grill's working partners), are huddled in the corner. Sullivan leans back on his stool and laces his fingers behind his head as he watches the door. Burns taps his foot and stays on the edge of his stool ready to spring up at any moment.

There have been many high points for The Delta Grill since it opened in December of 1997: a packed crowd on opening night; being named Manhattan's best

The two Toms, co-owners Tom Burns and Tom Sullivan (left)

"Ragin' with Cajun Flavor"

— NEW YORK DAILY NEWS

Cajun Restaurant by *New York Press* in 1998; great reviews from *The New York Daily News*, ("Ragin' with Cajun Flavor"), *New York Magazine*, (". . . miraculous exception to the norm"), and *Time Out New York*, ("portions are big, prices are easy . . ."). But tonight is a crowning moment. The etouffee on the proverbial pork chop.

At any moment, Chef Paul Prudhomme, the Cajun food king, arguably the most famous, and certainly the most acclaimed chef in America, will be coming through the heavy wooden front doors.

Of the 16,000 restaurants in New York City, Chef Paul has chosen to bring his party to The Delta Grill tonight not so much to check out his Cajun competition,

but to check-in on his protege, Greg Tatis. Tatis worked for Chef Paul at K. Paul's New York in 1988, (for one year of the restaurant's three-year run), then later at the famous K. Paul's in New Orleans' French Quarter for nearly eight years.

This is a night Greg has dreamed about. Every night except for last night, when he barely slept.

Greg paces the kitchen a few times, then he buttons up the top button of his white double-breasted chef's coat that he's wearing over his loose, sweatpants-like Chef's pants with the chili pepper print. He walks outside. He can see his breath in the late February night air. He rubs his hands together then suddenly, throws his arms out wide.

"Chef! Welcome!" he says, giving Chef Paul a bear hug. Greg shows Chef Paul's group to a comfortable, back corner table and passes out menus.

"Wow! Such a big menu!" Chef Paul says.

"It's New York," Greg says. "We gotta make everybody happy."

Tania Friese, an attractive brunette waitress with a long ponytail of curly hair, approaches the table to serve a first course of Coconut and Almond Battered Chicken. She confesses, "I was nervous when he first came in. But then I saw that he was shorter than me...and he was so nice."

"I have no idea where I'd be today without that man. He's an intricate part of my life —a huge part of my life."

— GREG TATIS ON CHEF PAUL PRUDHOMME

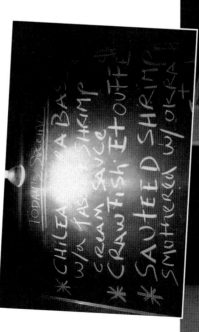

She soon returns confidently with an absolutely huge, heaping platter of ribs, porkchops and bronzed chicken.

Chef Paul looks up at Tania. "Hmm," he says. "It looks like Greg is skimping on the portions."

Tania laughs a Jennifer Tilley laugh and looks over her shoulder at Greg, who is peeking around the corner from the wooden phone booth just around the edge of the group's table. He crosses his arms in front of his chest and breaks into a grin. He then returns to the kitchen to prepare a sampling of each dessert on the menu, including sweet potato pecan pie, bananas foster and the chef's favorite, bread pudding. Tania brings them out.

"Sweet!" Greg says, doing a little hip-wiggling, one-man dance as he watches his desserts being devoured.

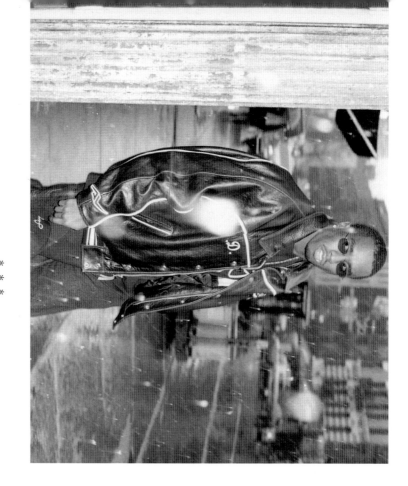

* * *

"New Orleans and New York City are the two greatest cities in the world," says Burns, who has lived in both. "Put them together and . . ."

"New Orleans is not just a cuisine, it's a subculture," says Sullivan. "You get the music, attitude and a great range of food."

"Plus," Burns says, "between 46th and 57th streets, there are nine Italian restaurants, 11 Chinese and fifty-something delis. Ninth Avenue needed us."

"New Orleans and New York City are the two greatest cities in the world."

—Tom Burns

The Delta Grill is a Cajun roadhouse-style restaurant and bar complete with an indoor corrugated tin awning, an old-fashioned wooden telephone booth and a series of lazy-paced ceiling fans connected by a rotating cable. Billie Holiday coos over the sound system by day, live Jazz gets feet tapping at night.

An after-work beer-drinking trio of businessmen, expecting to do the usual chicken wing thing, instead order an appetizer of fried green tomatoes with diced chicken in a black pepper cream sauce.

"Greg tries to hit on all four cylinders of the tongue," Burns says.

One of the businessmen says, "I don't know about cylinders. But those things rock!"

Denise Roerman, a pretty, blonde actress in her early thirties, sits at the bar waiting for her order of crab

The Delta Grill has thrived. People are attracted by the comfortable decor and laid back attitude of the staff, something not exactly synonymous with most, "What'll it be, Mac?" New York City establishments.

Many an unsuspecting Delta Grill patron has ventured inside expecting run-of-the-mill bar food or pretty decent Cajun fare. That's Chef Greg's chance to sneak in and blow them away.

It's all about the food.

"Food is Number One here," Greg says.

Like his teacher, Chef Paul, Greg believes presentation is important. But you won't see Greg crashing a slightly imperfect-looking plate to the floor in a tantrum.

"Like that whole nouvelle cuisine era of food really sucked. It looked great but $30 for three edible flower petals?" Greg says. "C'mon."

Flavorful comfort food that people can savor. But in New York City, more than anywhere else, they want it now.

"People expect a lot from a kitchen," he says. "A three-course meal in an hour."

cakes. Roerman is a St. Louis native: "A lot of people ask me if St. Louis is in Louisiana," she laughs. She and a friend are "Death of a Salesman"-bound but first...

"If crab cakes are on the menu," she says, "I have to have them. I'm obsessed." Her verdict: two enthusiastic, (her mouth is full), thumbs up. "These are way up there," she says. "The pecans are great. Mmmm! The texture!"

> "People expect a lot from a kitchen. A three-course meal in an hour."
>
> — CHEF GREG TATIS

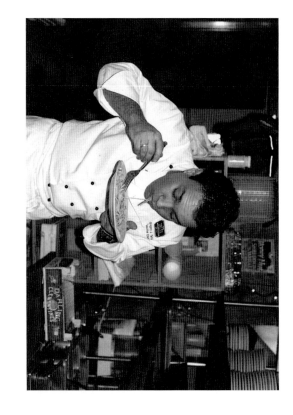

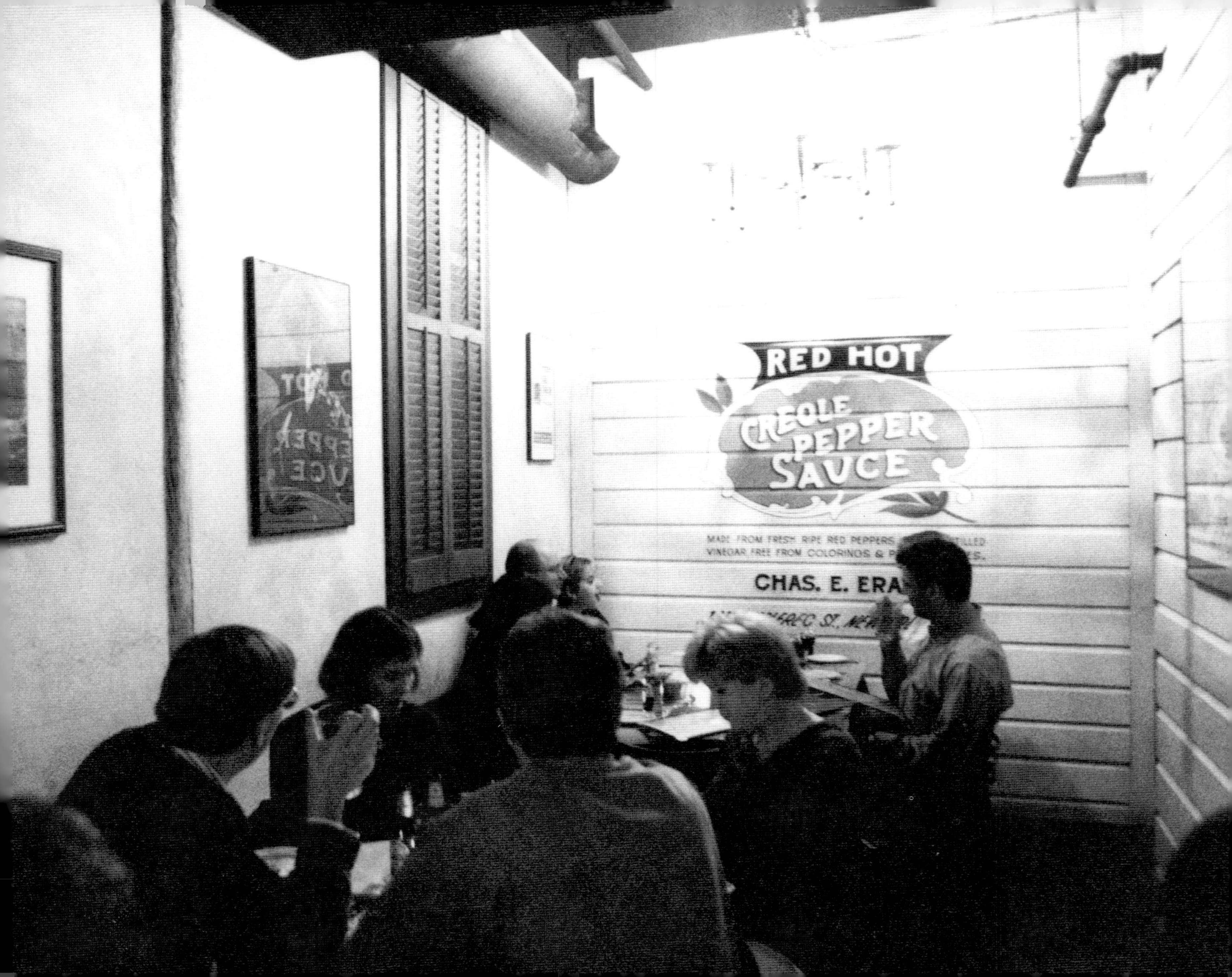
RED HOT
CREOLE PEPPER SAUCE
CHAS. E. ERA

But Greg does his best. "I genuinely want people to leave happy," he says.

He doesn't hide in his kitchen. (This would be difficult anyway since he works in full view of customers standing in line to use the bathrooms.) If someone sends something back, or even if they ask for a doggy bag, Greg charges out into the dining room to talk to the customer directly.

"Too many appetizers?" Chef Greg says to the doggy bag table. The group nods their heads "yes" in unison assuring him the food was great, they just couldn't eat another bite.

"Good," he grins. "Come back soon."

"When I see a packed crowd at the door, my heart races . . ."

— CHEF GREG

* * *

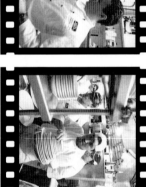

Greg Tatis grew up in Queens and always wanted to be a chef. He worked at several establishments before interviewing with Chef Paul when he came to open K. Paul's — New York in 1988.

"I would have done anything to work for him," Greg said.

Chef Paul began the interview by asking what kind of girls Greg liked and what he did for fun. He then turned serious. "What can you contribute?" he asked. Greg answered that he had been working for Steve Van Gelder, the chef at Nicolodean Restaurant in Queens, for five years.

"What if I told you everything Steve told you was wrong?" asked Chef Paul.

"I'd re-learn it," Greg said.

Chef Paul called the next day. Greg worked at K. Paul's — New York for one year before he was selected to move to New Orleans to work at the original K. Paul's, where he worked for seven and a half years.

"Nobody liked me in the beginning," Greg said. One assistant chef in particular would continually give the young New Yorker the longest "prep" list, sometimes

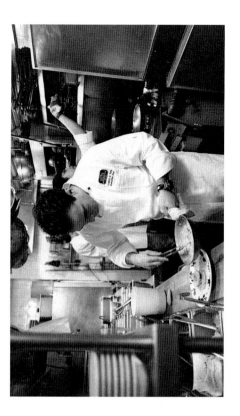

including five types of sauces such as oyster Hollandaise. Or another assistant would bark, "Fix that sauce!" Returning to check it, he would say, "Now, *that's* better!" (Greg chuckled to himself, since he had changed nothing.) Greg simply persisted. Peeling and chopping barrels of onions, bell peppers, garlic and parsley. He came in early because there was so much to do. Soon, he came to think of his K. Paul's co-workers as extended family.

"It's hard not to," Greg said, "when you're there all the time — sometimes 12 or 15 hours a day."

In his long hours working with Chef Paul, Greg took away two important things. First, *no kvetching*. During a trip to cater an event for a Children's Hospital in Pittsburgh,

Greg and his co-workers labored for days making some 300 "boats," six at a time made entirely of bread, sail and all. Each boat contained garlic seafood on the bow, etouffe in the mid-section and oyster cream sauce on the stern.

"It was out of control," Greg laughed. After three days of only three hours sleep per night, Greg began to complain. A lot. Chef Paul pulled him aside, "I know you're working hard, but stop complaining and go to work."

"You never stop learning — food is endless. There's no way that you know everything about food.

— Chef Greg

Greg said he never complained again. "Chef just thought, if you work, you work," he said.

Second, and probably most important, Greg gleaned his approach to food while working in New Orleans.

"Chef Paul has a huge understanding of food," Greg said. "How things react. What happens when you put things together. He's a master of depth. Start off with a good foundation and build layer by layer."

Greg said he approaches his own recipes in this way: caramelizing vegetables to bring out their sweetness before adding them to a recipe; roasting andouille or garlic first, rather than just chucking them into a gumbo.

"That's where the richness of flavor comes from," he said. "The dimension of taste where you take a bite and it finishes at the back of your throat."

Richness. Flavor. Foundation. Is this Cajun food? Doesn't Cajun mean blackened or burning hot?

"No way," Greg said.

As a matter of fact, some of Greg's recipes aren't blackened at all, but rather employ a technique known as bronzing, where an aluminum pan is used. The result is somewhat lighter than blackening, where a cast iron skillet is used.

"Cajun is the one true American type of food," Greg said, "because it was created here and combines Spanish, French, Creole, and African influences."

The meats, seafood, vegetables and spices traditionally used in Cajun cooking come from Louisiana (or from

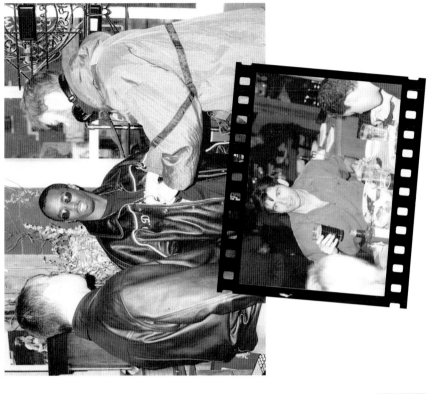

immigrants who brought them there). But the whole approach to Cajun cooking is unconventional, leaving room for creativity. And variety.

"That's what makes it fun," Greg said. "Cooking, especially Cajun cooking, is great because one person's interpretation of food is way different than someone else's. If everybody did it the same way we'd all be out of business." So here's one man's way. Your Shrimp Remoulade may not come out exactly like his.

"But it'll be great," he said. "That I can guarantee."

"I want people to sit back and go 'Damn! that was good!'"

— CHEF GREG

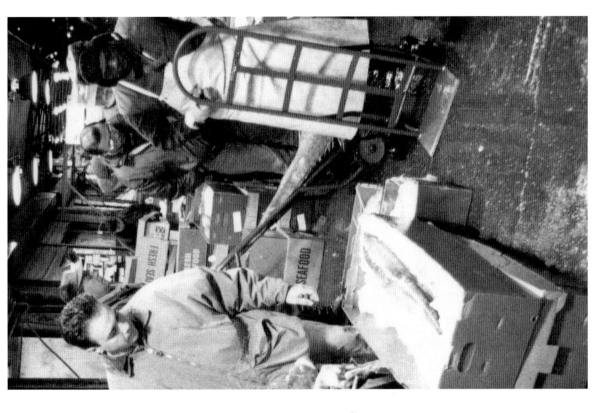

It's 4:40 AM on a blistery cold January morning. Nearly every Manhattan resident is still in bed. When their alarm clocks ring in three hours, many will shut them off, roll over and skip work due to a flu epidemic. But down at the Fulton Fish Market at South Street Seaport, hundreds of burly men in wool caps and leather jackets are already on the job, flu-like symptoms not withstanding. (Think *On the Waterfront* meets an Alka-Seltzer commercial.)

Chef Greg Tatis and Delta Grill co-owner Tom Burns pull up to the Fulton Market and park next to a truck with *Sonny's Seafood* painted in red.

They pass a group of men huddling around a barrel of burning plywood. The flames remind Tom of another fire, two years back. Mayor Guiliani had vowed to "clean up the docks" and eliminate alleged organized crime connections there. Dockworkers responded by burning all existing records. Tom flips up the collar on his coat.

Greg and Tom make their way over to the booths which represent different fish companies. They check out crate after crate of ice-packed fish. A photographer, a friend of the two, snaps a picture of Tom standing next to Greg, who is fingering the gill of a nice looking halibut.

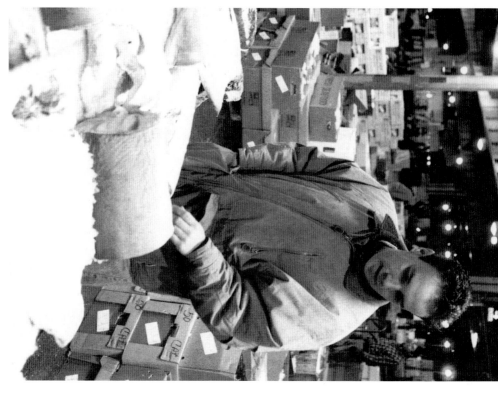

Greg seeks out a dealer he knows. He walks over to a group of men taking turns warming their hands in the orifice of a baudily-painted blow-up doll. He talks to one of the men, then motions to Tom and the photographer to join him.

The men are friendly. Greg has met them before.

Greg begins examining the wares of the blow-up doll group. He shows Tom the tricks he learned accompanying his mentor, Chef Paul Prudhomme, on fish market trips in Mexico.

"You have to watch for cloudy eyes, darkness in the gills, mucus and slimy skin," Greg says. "All bad signs." Greg said several times Chef Paul had him bite into raw fish to determine freshness. He said this was a common practice and the Mexican fisherman didn't seem to mind. Greg said this fish was too frozen to bite into and admitted that most days he skips this early morning trip altogether.

"Usually, I get my fish through a fish monger," Greg explains, as he flips over a flounder. "Actually, I use two. Then I can haggle."

So, if Chef Greg visits your table and says, "I have an excellent Chilean Sea Bass today," believe him.

Immediately, an Abe Pagoda look-a-like emerges. "The boss doesn't like it when you take pictures," he says in a low growl.

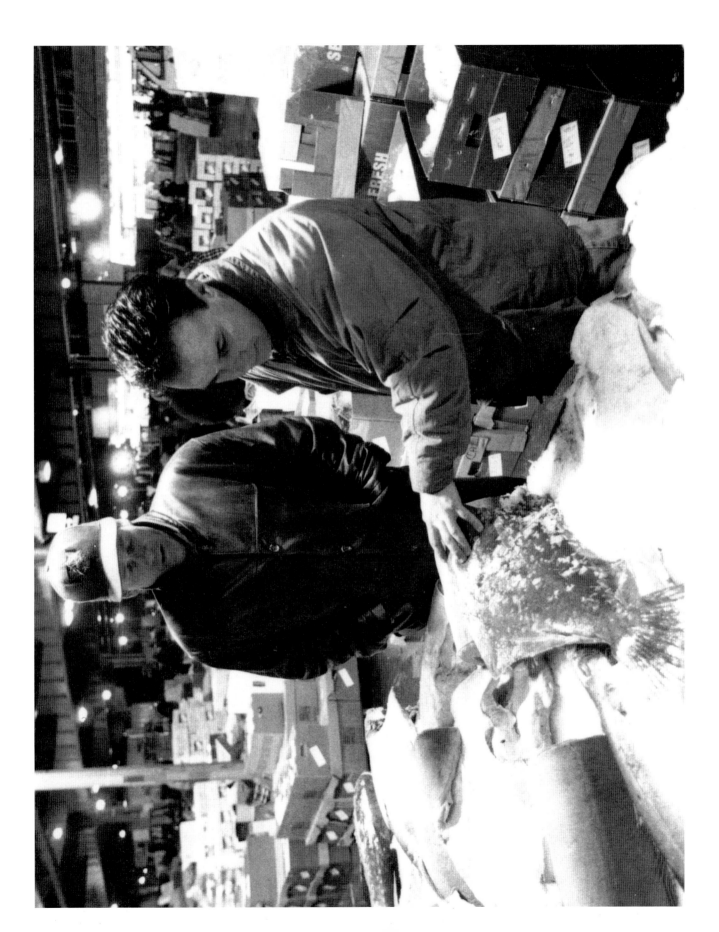

SEASONING MIXES

EQUIPMENT LIST

measuring cups and spoons
2 bowls
flour sifter
two 1-quart containers (for storing)
plate

SEASONING MIX #1 INGREDIENTS

¼ cup salt
4 tablespoons white pepper
4 tablespoons garlic powder
4 tablespoons onion powder
2 tablespoons cumin
2 tablespoons mustard powder
¾ cup paprika (Spanish)
2 tablespoons chili powder
4 tablespoons ground black pepper
½ teaspoon ground cayenne pepper

SEASONING MIX #2 INGREDIENTS

¼ cup salt
4 tablespoons white pepper
4 tablespoons garlic powder
4 tablespoons onion powder
2 tablespoons cumin
2 tablespoons mustard powder
¾ cup paprika (Spanish)
2 tablespoons chili powder
4 tablespoons ground black pepper
½ teaspoon ground cayenne pepper
2 tablespoons thyme (dry)
2 tablespoons basil (dry)
2 tablespoons oregano (dry)

So many people "season" simply by adding salt and pepper. They think Cajun spices are too hot. Greg created these seasoning mixes with this in mind. The combinations in these mixes are made to work with food, to make it flavorful, not just hot. They fill your whole mouth from the beginning of your first bite to your last swallow.

The quantities for the mix recipes are obviously enough for several recipes. Greg suggests you make them ahead of time (no need to stop in the middle of cooking a dish and make a seasoning mix!). Both mixes are great for adding zest to every day dishes. ("I dare ya!" Greg says. "Stash the salt for a week.")

Note: If there is a spice or herb you don't like, simply omit it from the recipe or you may substitute one of your own.

TO PREPARE SEASONING MIX #1 AND #2

Measure out all spices for Seasoning Mix #1 in bowl #1. Then place the sifter on a plate. Pour the seasonings from the bowl into the sifter. Next, lift up the sifter, place it over the bowl and sift all contents. Do this three times and put the bowl aside.

Next, measure out all spices for Seasoning Mix #2 in bowl #2. Place the sifter on a plate. Again, pour the seasonings from this bowl into the sifter. Note: the herbs from Seasoning Mix #2 will be left in the sifter. Just pour them back in the bowl when done. After sifting, mix both seasoning mixes separately with a spoon one last time for good luck, especially #2 because of the herbs.

When finished, place each mix in separate storage containers for later use.

CHICKEN STOCK

Many recipes call for chicken stock. Here is a homemade stock which may be made ahead of time. In fact, it'll have to be unless you want to wait eight hours to eat. If absolutely necessary, substitute canned stock.

TO PREPARE

COOK CHICKEN   Preheat oven to 550°. Take chicken backs or carcass and place in roasting pan. Place in oven and cook for 15 minutes.

PREP VEGGIES   While the backs are cooking, take 2 whole onions, ½ stock celery, 1 tomato and ½ pound carrots. Cut them into large (1") pieces. Wash all the veggies (except the tomato) in a colander. Remove the backs from the oven to check. They should be light brown. Rotate them in the pan, then add the veggies.

COOK AND BOIL   Return the pan to the oven for 20-25 minutes until backs are a rich brown. When done, remove the pan from the oven and pour 1 cup of water into the pan to deglaze. Stir up all the good stuff from the bottom and add contents of pan to a 8-quart stockpot. Add 1 gallon water and 1 tomato to the pot. Place pot on high flame and bring to a boil. When it comes to a boil, reduce flame immediately to a low simmer. Simmer for 8 hours. (Yes, 8 hours.) It's a lot of work, but freshly made stock is worth it.

FINISH   When stock is done, strain into a plastic (clear) container. When the fat settles at the top, ladle it off and discard. Divide stock into several smaller containers and freeze. Another option: cut the recipe in half and make a stronger stock which may be placed in an ice tray, frozen, and used by the cube. *Note: Cubes will be concentrated stock. Be sure to add water or canned stock before using.* (This idea was swiped from Chef Paul. It works great.)

EQUIPMENT LIST

roasting pan
chopping knife
cutting board
colander
8-quart stockpot
large spoon
ladle
plastic container(s)
ice tray

INGREDIENTS

6-8 pounds of chicken backs or carcass
1 gallon + 1 cup water
½ stock celery
2 whole onions
1 tomato
½ pound carrots
colander

ALLIGATOR SAUCE PIQUANT

So . . . does it taste like chicken? Greg says no. He describes this exotic Bayou meat as chewier than chicken, but not gamey. "It's got a seafoody taste towards the end," he says.

This delicacy presents the perfect opportunity to pay attention to your palette. "Eat it slow," Greg says. "There's a whole experience going on in your mouth."

Chicken. Shmicken.

EQUIPMENT LIST

measuring cups and spoons
chopping knife
spoon
4-quart pot
10" skillet
bowl

INGREDIENTS

¼ cup olive oil
3 cups medium diced onions
2 cups medium diced green bell pepper
1 cup medium diced celery
1 tablespoon fresh chopped garlic
3 tablespoons Seasoning Mix #2
28-ounce can whole peeled tomatoes
1 cup chicken stock
2 tablespoons finely diced jalapeño
1 pound alligator — diced small
1 tablespoon butter
white or brown rice (1 cup cooked per person)

TO PREPARE

SAUCE Add ¼ cup olive oil to a 4-quart pot and heat it on high. When it starts to smoke, add 3 cups medium diced onions, 2 cups medium diced green bell pepper, and 1 cup medium diced celery. Let the veggies sauté for 5 minutes then reduce the flame by half. Add 1 tablespoon fresh chopped garlic and 2 tablespoons Seasoning Mix #2 (see page 32). Continue to cook on a low flame for 10-15 more minutes, repeating a "stick and scrape" (let it cook, stick, then scrape the bottom and stir back into the vegetable mixture) as you go. Open one 28-ounce can whole peeled tomatoes. Crush the tomatoes with your hands or a fork, then add both tomatoes and their juice to vegetables. Next, add 1 cup chicken stock, and 2 tablespoons finely diced jalapeño. Let simmer on low flame.

ALLIGATOR Chop 1 pound alligator into small (not finely) diced pieces. Place in a bowl. Add 1 tablespoon Seasoning Mix #2. Mix thoroughly.

Take a 10" skillet, add 1 tablespoon butter and heat. When heated, add the alligator to the butter and sear it for about 2-3 minutes. When seared, pour the alligator and butter into the sauce and let simmer for one hour. Serve hot over white or brown rice. Serves 4.

ARTICHOKE WITH PORTABELLO MUSHROOMS AND CRAWFISH ETOUFEE

EQUIPMENT LIST

measuring cups and spoons
chopping knife
cutting board
large spoon
8–10" skillet (at least 2" deep)
4–6-quart pot
tongs
large mixing bowl
small bowl
whip
coffee cup

INGREDIENTS

3 cups medium diced onions
2 cups medium diced green bell pepper
2 cups medium diced celery
2 cups corn oil
2½ cups flour
1 tablespoon Seasoning Mix #1
2 tablespoons Worcestershire sauce
two 24-count artichokes
1 lemon, sliced
ice cubes
2 tablespoons margarine
1 tablespoon fresh chopped garlic
2 tablespoons Seasoning Mix #2
½ pound crawfish
2 cups sliced portabello mushrooms
2 cups chicken stock
1 tablespoon corn starch
2 tablespoons warm water
¼ cup sliced scallions

TO PREPARE

DARK ROUX   (Note: preparing roux is kind of intense — the oil gets hot and bubbly and everything moves quickly. Don't be intimidated! Hang in there.) Chop 1 cup medium diced onions, 1 cup medium diced green bell pepper and 1 cup medium diced celery. Set aside.

Heat 2 cups corn oil in an 8-10" skillet (at least 2" deep) over a high flame until it begins to smoke. When smoke appears, slowly add 2½ cups flour, using a whip to stir as you go. Don't stop stirring! Flour will turn a dark, rich brown after 10-15 minutes. Remove skillet from heat and stir in vegetables (above.), 1 tablespoon Seasoning Mix #1 (see page 32) and 2 tablespoons Worcestershire sauce. Set aside, but keep warm.

ARTICHOKES   Take two 24-count artichokes and cut ¼" off bottoms and ½" off the top.

Place them in a 4–6-quart pot and cover with water. Bring to a boil. Slice 1 lemon in half. Squeeze in all the juice, then drop the lemon halves into the water. Continue boiling until artichokes are tender (approximately 25 minutes). To check: grab an artichoke with a set of tongs. Remove a leaf from the center (near the heart) of the artichoke. If it comes out effortlessly, the artichoke is done.

Remove artichokes from pot. Place into a large bowl filled with 2 trays of ice and 2 cups water. Quickly remove artichokes from ice bath and place on a plate. Pull off each leaf, all the way down to the heart. Place them in a bowl and put in the refrigerator.

Place the hearts on a plate. Take a spoon and scoop out the hair which is on top of the heart. Be careful not to go into meat of the heart. Next, cut the hearts into slices, put them in a small bowl and set in the refrigerator.

CRAWFISH ETOUFEE   Heat 4–6-quart pot on a medium flame. Add 2 tablespoons margarine and let it melt. Add 2 cups medium diced onions, 1 cup medium diced green bell pepper, 1 cup medium diced celery, 1 tablespoon fresh chopped garlic, and 2 tablespoons Seasoning Mix #2 (see page 32). Sauté for 20-25 minutes. Then add ½ pound crawfish, 2 cups sliced portabello mushrooms and stir. Cook an additional 5 minutes, continuing to stir.

Continued on page 38

ARTICHOKE WITH PORTABELLO MUSHROOMS AND CRAWFISH ETOUFEE

(continued)

Add 2 cups chicken stock. Bring to a simmer. Then, take 1 tablespoon roux, and ½ cup chicken stock (from the simmering pot), place in bowl and stir together. Then add that mixture back to the pot. Bring to a boil. Cook an additional 5-6 minutes.

Next, add 1 tablespoon corn starch and 2 tablespoons warm water into a coffee cup. Stir together, then add to pot. To finish, add artichoke hearts to sauce with ¼ cup sliced scallions. Stir and continue to simmer.

RETURN TO ARTICHOKES Fill 4–6-quart pot halfway with water. Heat the pot on a medium flame. Scoop artichoke leaves into pot and heat them 2-3 minutes. Scoop leaves out of the water and arrange them in a circle on a large plate, as if the leaves were the petals on a flower.

SERVE Pour sauce over leaves on the plate and serve warm. *Serves 4.*

FRIED CHEESE GRITS WITH CHICKEN CREOLE SAUCE

EQUIPMENT LIST

measuring cups and spoons
chopping knife
roasting pan or sheet pan (13" x 9" x 2")
4-quart pot (short and wide)
10" skillet
8" sauté pan
plastic wrap
coffee cup or round cookie cutter
3 bowls
candy or oil thermometer

INGREDIENTS

2 cups instant grits
½ tablespoon black pepper
1 tablespoon salt
4 tablespoons butter
3 cups grated sharp cheddar cheese
3 tablespoons margarine
3 cups chopped onions
1 cup bell peppers
1 cup medium diced celery
1 tablespoon garlic
3 tablespoons Seasoning Mix #2
1 cup chicken stock
28-ounce can whole peeled tomatoes and
   their juice
1 tablespoon dark brown sugar
1 pound diced (½" chunks) chicken breasts
2 eggs
¼ cup milk
2 cups flour
2 cups unseasoned bread crumbs
2 cups corn oil

TO PREPARE

Grits are a southern staple. Most people jazz up these dullish morning carbohydrates with butter and salt. But Greg has another way. His secret: lots of cheese. Then, he fries them, so they don't get mushy. Top the grits with this incredible sauce. Grits . . . they're not just for breakfast anymore.

PREPPING CHEESE GRITS

Cheese Grits should be made first since they need time to chill. *Hint: This step may be done a day ahead so the grits could be fried while the Chicken Creole Sauce is cooking.* (Estimated cooking time: 5-7 minutes.)

Take 4-quart pot, add 8 cups water and bring to a boil. While waiting for water to boil, take a roasting pan or sheet pan (13" x 9" x 2"), and line it with plastic wrap, covering the pan completely. When water boils, add 2 cups grits, ½ tablespoon black pepper, 1 tablespoon salt, 4 tablespoons butter and 2 cups grated sharp cheddar cheese. Reduce the flame by half and stir continuously. Use the spoon to break up any clumps.

When grits begin to thicken and turn orange, remove from flame and fold in last cup grated cheese. Then pour grits into lined roasting pan and set in refrigerator. (Grits will harden.) Chill at least one hour.

CHICKEN CREOLE SAUCE

(Estimated total cooking time: 35 minutes.) Heat a 4-quart pot on a high flame. Add 2 tablespoons margarine and melt. When margarine melts, add 3 cups chopped onions, 1 cup bell peppers and 1 cup medium diced celery. Add 1 tablespoon garlic, and 2 tablespoons Seasoning Mix #2 *(see page 32).*

Then, caramelize ingredients inside the pot. At the 8-minute mark the sticking will begin. Stick and scrape: Let it stick, then scrape the bottom of the pot, getting all the good stuff up from the bottom of the pot into your vegetables. Continue to do this for another 4-5 minutes. Add 1 cup chicken stock to deglaze the bottom of the pot.

Continued on page 42

FRIED CHEESE GRITS WITH CHICKEN CREOLE SAUCE

(continued)

Once deglazed, lower flame by half. Then open one 28-ounce can whole peeled tomatoes. Pour the juice into the pot. Then crush the tomatoes (using a fork or your hand), and add them to the sauce. Add 1 tablespoon dark brown sugar (or white sugar if preferred).

When the sauce returns to a simmer, reduce the flame by one quarter. Continue to cook the sauce slowly over a low flame.

Place 1 pound diced (½" chunks) chicken breasts in a bowl and stir in 1 tablespoon Seasoning Mix #2, covering chicken thoroughly. (*Note: Chicken should weigh 1 pound after skin and bones are removed.*)

Heat an 8" sauté pan on a medium flame. Add 1 tablespoon margarine and let it melt. When melted, add chicken and brown it off. No need to cook all the way; simply brown it on the outside, 2-3 minutes. Then, add it to the Creole Sauce. Set it aside on a cool burner.

FRYING   Remove grits from refrigerator, turn pan upside down and flip the solid "rectangle" out onto a cutting board. Peel away the plastic wrap. Take a coffee cup or round cookie cutter and stamp out circle-shaped cakes from the grits. *Hint: visualize cutting circles in Playdough* (makes 9).

Take 3 bowls. In bowl #1, whip together 2 eggs and ¼ cup milk until frothy. In bowl #2, add 2 cups flour. In bowl #3, add 2 cups unseasoned bread crumbs. Bread each cake by dipping it in bowl #1, then #2, then #3. Cover completely. Set on a plate.

Take a 10" skillet, add 2 cups oil and heat to 325°. Fry 4 cakes at a time, approximately 2 minutes on each side, until golden brown. Remove when finished and place cakes on paper towel. Cover with another paper towel and continue. When finished, discard paper towels and place all fried cakes on a platter. Pour Chicken Creole Sauce on top. Serve hot.
Serves 4.

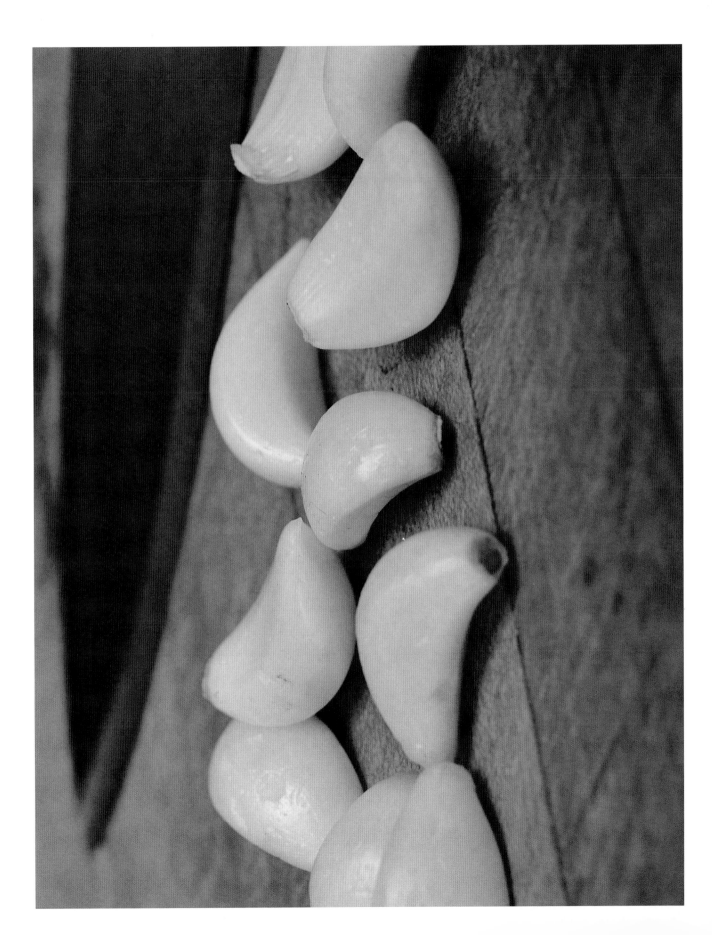

ROASTED PECAN CRAB CAKES WITH SAFFRON SAUCE

EQUIPMENT LIST

measuring cups and spoons
chopping knife
cutting board
mallet
10" skillet
2 plates
3 bowls
large spoon
whip
paper towels (about 5 sheets)
sheet pan
food processor (or knife)
spatula

INGREDIENTS

2 cups pecan halves
1 tablespoon butter
2 tablespoons olive oil
1 cup finely diced onions
¼ cup finely diced yellow or red bell pepper
¼ cup finely diced green bell pepper
2 tablespoons fresh chopped garlic
3 tablespoons Seasoning Mix #2
1 pound jumbo lump crab meat
2 tablespoons mayonnaise
1 tablespoon Creole mustard (or a favorite mustard)
1 cup flour
2 eggs
¼ cup milk
2 cups peanut oil

Why are these crab cakes the best in the Big Apple or the Big Easy? It's the crab meat. 100% real crab meat. No fillers or bread crumbs. At the Delta Grill, it's the real deal. They've got spices, but the crab taste still comes through . . . and the pecans . . . and the saffron sauce. Forget about it!

TO PREPARE

ROASTING THE PECANS   Preheat oven to 450°. Take pecans and spread them evenly on a sheet pan. Place them in the oven and roast until they are light brown. The pecans should be in little chunks. Be careful and using a mallet, pound them into small pieces. The pecans should be in little chunks. Be careful not to go too far — you don't want powder! Place the pecans in a bowl and set them aside.

COOK VEGGIES   Heat a 10" skillet on a medium flame. Add 1 tablespoon butter and 2 tablespoons olive oil. Heat until they are melted. Then, add 1 cup finely diced onions, ¼ cup finely diced red or yellow bell pepper, ¼ cup finely diced green bell pepper, 1 tablespoon chopped garlic and 1 table-spoon Seasoning Mix #2 *(see page 32)*. Sauté until they are light brown (approximately 10 minutes). Veggies should be crunchy to taste. When done, place veggies on a plate and put in refrigerator.

PREP CRAB CAKES   Take the crab meat, place it on a plate and pick through it for shells. This will take some time but it's important. Nobody wants to eat shells! It works best to take a little crab meat in your hand, feel for the shells, remove them with your other hand, then place "cleaned" meat to the other side of plate. Keep going until finished.

Take cleaned crab meat, place it in a bowl and combine it with 2 tablespoons mayonnaise, 1 tablespoon Creole mustard, 1 tablespoon Seasoning Mix #2, 1 tablespoon garlic, and the cooled veggie mix. Mix thoroughly. Then make 2-ounce patties with the mixture and place them on a plate (makes approximately 10 cakes). When finished, place the plate in the refrigerator.

BREADING   Set up for breading: take the flour and combine it in bowl #3 with 1 tablespoon Seasoning Mix #2. Mix together. Then take 2 eggs and ¼ cup milk and whip them in Bowl #2. Then take pecans (already in bowl #1) and get ready to bread your cakes. Take one cake at a time and softly dip it in each bowl. Go from flour to eggs to pecans and place on plate. Do this to all the cakes. Make sure each cake is completely, but lightly, covered with the flour, then the eggs, or the pecans won't stick!

Continued on page 46

ROASTED PECAN CRAB CAKES WITH SAFFRON SAUCE

(continued)

(*Note: If planning to serve Crab Cakes with Saffron Sauce, proceed to next recipe, make sauce, keep warm, then return to this recipe and prepare to fry.*)

FRYING   Heat the skillet on a medium flame. Add 2 cups peanut oil and heat an additional 3 to 4 minutes. When heated (approximately 325°), place several crab cakes at a time in the oil. Cook on each side for about 3 minutes (use a spatula to flip), then place cakes on a plate lined with paper towels, 2 on a plate and one paper towel for each layer. When done frying, serve plain or with Saffron Sauce. *Serves 5-10.*

TO PREPARE THE SAFFRON SAUCE

EQUIPMENT LIST

measuring cups and spoons
1-quart sauce pan
whip
coffee cup

INGREDIENTS

1 cup chicken stock
1 cup heavy cream
1 tablespoon Seasoning Mix #1
2 pinches saffron
1 tablespoon corn starch
2 tablespoons warm water

Take a sauce pan, add 1 cup chicken stock and 1 cup heavy cream and bring to a boil. Stir with a large spoon. Add 2 pinches saffron and 1 tablespoon Seasoning Mix #1 (*see page 32*). Simmer for about 5 minutes. (*Note: When cooking cream, watch closely. It has a tendency to boil over.*)

While the sauce is simmering, mix 1 tablespoon corn starch and 2 tablespoons warm water together in a coffee cup until smooth. (*Note: Greg uses his fingers to make sure there are no clumps.*) Then add to pot slowly until sauce is a little thick. (*It should pour smoothly off a spoon.*)

Serve hot with crab cakes.

FRIED GREEN TOMATOES WITH BLACK PEPPER ENVY SAUCE

Fried Green Tomatoes, a southern classic, are one of the most popular items on The Delta Grill menu. Yes, Greg saw the movie, "Fried Green Tomatoes at the Whistle Stop Cafe." He claims he didn't cry so he be paid attention: he said the actors coated their tomatoes the same way he does with traditional breading (corn meal, corn flour, regular flour).

Greg says not too many New Yorkers get Fried Green Tomatoes and not too many people, even Southerners "get 'em good." Green tomatoes taste different than red; they're tangier and have a different texture.

New Yorkers go nuts over Greg's sauce which he drapes over his tomatoes and serves as an appetizer. "I think it's the black pepper," he says.

TO PREPARE

PREPARE TOMATOES   Take the 4 tomatoes and tomato shark (knife) and cut out the core on top and bottom of tomatoes. Be careful to take out just the core and not the meat of the tomato. Now place tomatoes on the cutting board. Take a knife and slice tomatoes ½-inch thick. Place on a plate and set aside.

Take 3 tablespoons of Seasoning Mix #1 *(see page 32)* and sprinkle on both sides of each tomato and set on plate #2 and set aside.

BREADING   Take the 2 bowls. In bowl #1, combine the corn flour, cornmeal, flour and ½ table-spoon of Seasoning Mix #1. Mix thoroughly with a spoon. Then in bowl #2, place 3 eggs and water and whip them together until smooth and airy. Now, taking one tomato at a time, first dip it into the egg mix, then into the flour mix, finishing by placing it on a plate. Be careful not to get too much breading on your tomatoes — they should be covered evenly but lightly. (If part of the tomato has no breading, then simply dip it back in the egg mix, then flour mix again, but only the part that is not breaded.)

(Note: If planning to smother Fried Green Tomatoes with Black Pepper Envy Sauce, proceed to next recipe, make sauce, then prepare to fry.)

FRYING   Now the fun part! Take the 10" skillet and place it on the stove. Turn the burner on medium heat and add the corn oil. (It should take about 5 minutes to get to temperature.) The oil must be hot before frying to ensure that tomatoes will be crispy and not oily tasting.

Continued on page 50

EQUIPMENT LIST

measuring cups and spoons
chopping knife
cutting board
"tomato shark" knife (optional)
2 sheet pans or plates
2 bowls
spoon
whip or fork
8" or 10" frying pan
paper towels (about 5 sheets)

INGREDIENTS

4 green tomatoes
3½ tablespoons Seasoning Mix #1
½ cup corn flour
½ cup cornmeal
¼ cup flour
3 eggs
2 teaspoons water
2 cups corn oil

FRIED GREEN TOMATOES WITH BLACK PEPPER ENVY SAUCE

(continued)

Now fill the skillet with the tomatoes and cook them on each side, about 1½ minutes a side, then place on a plate that has been lined with the paper towels. (Take 2 sheets for the bottom and one sheet between each layer of tomatoes.) That's it. Cover with Black Pepper Envy Sauce or serve them plain. Your choice. *Serves 4.*

TO PREPARE THE BLACK PEPPER ENVY SAUCE

EQUIPMENT LIST

measuring spoons and cups
chopping knife
cutting board
large spoon
2-quart sauce pan
bowl
coffee cup

INGREDIENTS

½ pound chicken in ¼" diced cubes
1 tablespoon Seasoning Mix #1
2 tablespoons olive oil
1 cup shiitake mushrooms (¼ inch slices)
½ tablespoon fresh chopped garlic
1 teaspoon ground black pepper
1 cup chicken stock
½ cup heavy cream
½ cup sliced scallions (¼ inch slices)
1 tablespoon corn starch
2 tablespoons water

PREP CHICKEN   Take ½ pound diced chicken, 1 tablespoon Seasoning Mix #1, and place in bowl. Mix thoroughly until chicken is completely covered with seasoning. Set aside.

COOK SAUCE   Heat a 2-quart saucepan on a high flame. Add 2 tablespoons olive oil. When oil starts to smoke (about 2 minutes), add ½ pound diced chicken and sauté until brown (another 2 minutes). Next, add 1 cup shiitake mushrooms (¼ inch slices), ½ tablespoon fresh chopped garlic and 1 teaspoon ground black pepper. Reduce flame by half and sauté for another 2 minutes.

Deglaze pot by pouring in chicken stock and scraping all that good stuff up from the bottom of the pot with a spoon. (It's important not to leave that sticky stuff behind — it has all the seasonings and flavor!) Then add ½ cup heavy cream and ½ cup scallions (chopped in ¼-inch slices). Stir and bring to a boil.

Continued on page 51

Then, take a coffee cup and mix 1 tablespoon corn starch and 2 tablespoons warm water. Mix until smooth. When the sauce reaches a boil, stir in the corn starch mixture. Keep stirring until sauce thickens. It should be a smooth consistency. If it gets too thick just add a little more chicken stock.

SERVE Pour the sauce over Fried Green Tomatoes and serve immediately.

FRIED GREEN TOMATOES WITH BLACK PEPPER ENVY SAUCE

LOBSTER DUMPLINGS WITH MANGO SAUCE

EQUIPMENT LIST

measuring cups and spoons
chopping knife
cutting board
6-quart pot
6-8 inch skillet
bowl
large spoon
pastry brush
2-quart pot (short and wide)
fine strainer
large serving plate
food processor

INGREDIENTS

one 1½ pound lobster
2 tablespoons olive oil
½ cup finely diced onions
½ cup finely diced red bell pepper
½ tablespoon fresh chopped garlic
2 tablespoons Seasoning Mix #2
¼ cup finely diced scallions
2 tablespoons toasted sesame oil
2 tablespoons flour
6 sheets egg roll wrappers
1 egg
2 tablespoons olive oil
½ cup medium diced red bell pepper
½ cup medium diced onions
1 teaspoon fresh chopped garlic
2 ripe mangoes
1 cup chicken stock
¼ cup heavy cream

TO PREPARE

COOK LOBSTER Fill a 6-quart pot with water and bring it to a boil. Place lobster in water and cook for 15-20 minutes. Remove, place on plate and into refrigerator to cool for ½ hour.

COOK VEGGIES While the lobster is cooling, take 2 tablespoons olive oil and heat in a 6-8 inch skillet until hot. When skillet is heated, add ½ cup finely diced onions, ½ cup finely diced red bell pepper, ½ tablespoon fresh chopped garlic and ½ tablespoon Seasoning Mix # 2 (*see page 32*). Cook veggies until they're done, but still crunchy (about 15 minutes). Place on a plate, and set in refrigerator for 15 minutes.

PREP LOBSTER / MIX While veggies are cooling, take lobster and cut the tail off just above the fan. Then cut the head by making a diagonal cut from the top of the head down. (Heads up! This will be used as a garnish.) Then remove all remaining meat from lobster. Chop the meat into fine pieces and place in a bowl.

Take cooled veggies from the refrigerator and stir into the bowl with lobster. Also add ½ tablespoon Seasoning Mix #2, ¼ cup scallions, and 2 tablespoons toasted sesame oil. Mix together with a large spoon.

STUFFING Take a plate and dust it with 2 tablespoons flour. Set aside.

Take 6 sheets egg roll wrappers. Cut them in half on a cutting board. Then cut them in half again so there are 4 squares from each sheet.

Taking 1 square at a time, scoop 1 teaspoon of the lobster / veggie mixture in the center of each square.

Then, take a bowl and break 1 egg into it. Whip vigorously until egg yoke and white are combined. Then take a pastry brush, dip it into the bowl and brush some of the egg on the edge of one square. Next, take each corner of the square, and use fingers to pinch it together and twist. Seal it tightly! There should be no gaps. Last, finish each dumpling by brushing the top with more egg. Repeat for all squares.

Continued on page 54

LOBSTER DUMPLINGS WITH MANGO SAUCE

(continued)

As each dumpling is finished, set it on the flour-covered plate. Makes 20-25 dumplings.

COOK DUMPLINGS   Take a 2-quart pot (short and wide), and fill almost to the top with water. Place a fine strainer on top of the pot and bring water to a boil. Once water is boiling, place 6 dumplings at a time into the strainer and cook for 2 minutes.

Remove strainer from pot. Gently pour dumplings onto a plate. Try not to touch them — they are extremely delicate! Cover with foil to keep dumplings hot until sauce is done.

MANGO SAUCE   Heat 2-quart pot on a medium flame. Add 2 tablespoons olive oil. When hot, add ½ cup red bell peppers, ½ cup onions, 1 teaspoon fresh chopped garlic and 1 tablespoon Seasoning Mix #2. Simmer.

While veggies are cooking, peel 2 ripe mangoes. Remove all the meat away from the pits and dice into 1" chunks. When veggies have been cooking for 15 minutes, add the mango chunks. After 3 minutes, stir in 1 cup chicken stock. Cook for another 10 minutes until the mango chunks are soft. Remove from stove. Scoop into a food processor and grind until smooth. Then, scoop mixture back into the pot. Add ¼ cup heavy cream and return to simmer.

SERVE   Using a large serving plate, place the lobster tail and head in center for a garnish, then surround with dumplings. Top with mango sauce and serve warm. *Serves 2-4.*

STUFFED MIRLITON WITH SHRIMP HOLLANDAISE

Mirlitons are pear-shaped squash from Mexico (also called chayote) which are widely used in Louisiana kitchens. Greg likes to use them because they have a "cucumbery" texture which cools the palette and evens out the zing of a particularly zesty sauce.

TO PREPARE

MIRLITONS Cut 2 mirlitons in half lengthwise. Add to a 2-quart saucepan and cover with water. Heat the saucepan on a high flame. Bring to a boil. Continue boiling until mirlitons are soft and tender (20-25 minutes). While the "mirls" are cooking, make the Hollandaise.

HOLLANDAISE Heat another 2-quart saucepan on a low flame. Add ½ pound butter and melt slowly. (The goal is to separate not to emulsify.) Cooking too fast will result in the butter mixing together instead of separating. Your result should consist of 3 layers — buttermilk, which rests on the bottom, the butter fat, which rests in between and a light thin layer on top. Slow, slow, slow . . .

Next, separate 3 eggs, and place just the yolks in a 2-quart mixing bowl. (Discard the whites.) Add ¼ teaspoon Seasoning Mix #1 *(see page 32)*. Add 3 tablespoons white wine, and 1 tablespoon Worcestershire Sauce. Squeeze the juice of ½ lemon and add it also. *(Be careful not to get any seeds in the sauce! Use your hand or a citrus squeezer — Greg uses his hands.)*

Check butter. Set it aside in a warm place. The stove is fine (with burner turned off). Do not rest it where it will get cold — that could cause the butter to congeal.

BACK TO THE MIXING BOWL Take a whip and break up the yolks, then mix contents of the bowl thoroughly, working air into the mixture until the consistency is nice and frothy. *(Note: Bowl will be used as the top of a double boiler. It should be a size to fit snugly on top of the saucepan.)*

Next, take a saucepan and add a small amount of water (approximately 1 inch). Bring to a boil. Then set up double boiler: grab the bowl using a napkin or potholder and rest it on top of the saucepan. Proceed to cook the eggs (using the steam rising from the saucepan) for the Hollandaise (approximately 2 minutes).

Continued on page 58

EQUIPMENT LIST

measuring cups and spoons
chopping knife
three 2-quart saucepans
10" skillet for frying
3 mixing bowls
2 plates, 1 serving platter
candy or oil thermometer

INGREDIENTS

2 mirlitons
½ pound unsalted butter
3 eggs
¼ teaspoon Seasoning Mix #1
3 tablespoons white wine
1 tablespoon Worcestershire sauce
juice of 1 lemon
8 shrimp (16-20 count, peeled, cleaned and de-veined)
2 cups sliced shiitake mushrooms (tightly packed)
1 tablespoon fresh chopped garlic
½ cup sliced scallions
1 tablespoon margarine
¼ cup Worcestershire Sauce
½ cup chicken stock
½ cup flour
2 tablespoons, 1 teaspoon Seasoning Mix #2
2 eggs
1 tablespoon water
¼ cup + 2 tablespoons milk
1 cup unseasoned bread crumbs
2 cups corn oil
2 tablespoons butter

STUFFED MIRLITON WITH SHRIMP HOLLANDAISE

(continued)

IMPORTANT Watch for lumps, which means the eggs are cooking too fast. If lumps appear, temporarily pull the bowl from heat to reduce temperature, but keep stirring. This is a slow process. Take your time — you don't want scrambled eggs!

The eggs will become light and frothy and lose their strong egg taste as the sauce begins to thicken, usually within 2-3 minutes. It's very important to continuously whip them until done! Don't leave sauce unattended. Desired result: a meringue consistency — running a whip through it should produce little peaks. When it gets to that point, pull it off the heat.

Next, place the bowl containing the eggs on top of the napkin or potholder (to keep it steady while pouring butter into it). Very slowly, add all the butter to the egg mixture. Use a ladle if you like. (*Hint: get someone to help* — *they can hold the bowl while you pour!*) Remember not to pour too fast or the Hollandaise may break. Also important: the butter should be temperate, not too hot.

You've got Hollandaise! Feel free to personalize sauce with mushrooms, some chopped shrimp or fresh basil or parsley for color! Cover with plastic wrap to keep it fresh. Set aside.

BACK TO THE MIRLS (which have been cooking 25 minutes). When done, they should be "fork tender," a fork will run directly through them with no force. Be careful not to overcook them! Their "meat" will be scooped out and used later.

Remove pot from the stove. Then, strain the mirls under hot water. Return them to the empty pot and chill by covering them with cold water. Then, immediately add 2 trays of ice. Get a spoon, and stir them so they begin to cool right away. This is important! Otherwise they will continue to cook on the inside.

Once chilled, peel the backs and take the skin off — on the inside there is a seed which should be removed. Also, at the very bottom of the mirl, the skin extends inside by the seed just a little bit. Peel this skin, too.

Next, take a spoon and scoop out the inside of each mirl, very gently as if making a little pirouge (boat). Scrape the inside of the hole, going a little deep. Cut scooped out piece in half. Place the scooped out "meat" on a plate. Take the mirls, set them on a plate and put both plates in the refrigerator.

THE STUFFING SAUCE Get a bowl. Throw in 8 shrimp (peeled, cleaned and de-veined). Add 1 teaspoon Seasoning Mix #2 (*see page 32*) into the bowl. Using hands, mix shrimp and seasoning together, covering them completely. In the same bowl, add the mirliton meat, 2 cups sliced shiitake mushrooms (tightly packed), one tablespoon fresh chopped garlic, and ½ cup sliced scallions. Stir ingredients with a spoon.

Continued on page 59

Next, heat a 2-quart saucepan on medium heat. Add 1 tablespoon margarine. When melted (about 2 minutes), pour the contents of the bowl into the saucepan and stir. When the shrimp begin to turn pink, add 1 tablespoon Seasoning Mix #2. Next, add the juice of ½ lemon, ¼ cup Worcestershire Sauce and ½ cup chicken stock.

Reduce temperature and simmer for approximately 1 minute. Stir in 2 tablespoons butter. The sauce will begin to emulsify; then it will take on a nice, creamy, consistency. Turn off the burner, but leave the pot on the stove to keep warm.

BREADING THE MIRLS

Take three bowls. Fill bowl #1 with ½ cup flour, ½ tablespoon Seasoning Mix #2 and blend together. Fill bowl #2 with 2 eggs, ¼ cup water, 2 tablespoons milk and whip them together. Fill bowl #3 with 1 cup unseasoned bread crumbs, ½ tablespoon Seasoning Mix #2 and blend. Set up the bowls three in a row. Take the mirl pirouges from the refrigerator and dip each piece one at a time into bowl #1, then #2, then #3. (Note: *Use one hand for the two "dry" bowls, #1 & #3, and the other hand for the wet bowl, #2.*) Cover the mirlitons completely but keep each layer thin. When finished, place them on a plate.

FRYING

Take a 10" skillet. Add 2 cups corn oil and heat approximately 4 minutes (to 325°). (*Hint: clean up while oil is heating — less work later! Unless, of course, you have suckered someone into cleaning up for you.*)

Sprinkle a few bread crumbs into oil to test heat. It's important to have an even heat when frying. Not too hot (this will result in burning) and not too cold (oil will seep into food).

Take mirls from plate and use tongs to place them in pot for 2½ to 3 minutes, until they are light golden brown. Line the plate with paper towels, and place mirls on plate when done. Then, take another paper towel and pat the top of the mirls. Make sure the pirouge side, (the scooped out side), is facing down so oil can drip out.

Place mirls on a serving platter. Reheat Stuffing Sauce and Hollandaise. Bring to a simmer, then prepare to stuff!

First remove the shrimps from sauce. Place two shrimp in each mirl. Then, spoon the remaining stuffing evenly over the shrimp. Then, top each mirl with 2-3 tablespoons Hollandaise. Serve any extra sauce on the side!
Serves 4.

FRIED OKRA

Whistle Dixie while you make this dish. Or New York, New York. Either way, watch people snap up this appetizer.

EQUIPMENT LIST

measuring cups and spoons
chopping knife
cutting board
4–6-quart pot (short and wide)
candy or oil thermometer
2 paper bags (small sandwich bags)
2-quart bowl
plate
paper towels
slotted spoon
whip

INGREDIENTS

4 cups fresh sliced okra
1 cup flour
2 tablespoons Seasoning Mix #2
3 eggs
1 cup milk
6½ cups corn oil
½ cup Creole mustard
3 tablespoons Worcestershire
1 teaspoon sugar
⅛ cup orange juice
½ cup cornmeal
1 cup corn flour

TO PREPARE

PREP OKRA Take 4 cups fresh sliced okra. (First, snip off the ends and top. Discard. Then, cut the middle part into ½" thick pieces.)

BREADING *(Hint: it's like Shake n' Bake.)* Take 2 paper bags and a 2-quart bowl. To bag #1: add 1 cup flour and ½ tablespoon Seasoning Mix #2. To bag #2: add ½ tablespoon Seasoning Mix #2 *(see page 32)*. To the bowl: add 3 eggs, 1 cup milk and ½ tablespoon Seasoning Mix #2. Whip together. To bag #2: add ½ cup flour, ½ cup corn meal, 1 cup corn flour and ½ tablespoon Seasoning Mix #2.

Place okra in bag #1 (2 cups at a time), twist the top of the bag and shake it up good. Open bag, reach in, remove okra and dip it in the egg wash. (This is going to get messy.) Then, place okra in bag #2, again twist the top of the bag and shake it up good. Using hands, remove okra and place onto a plate. Set aside.

FRYING Make a mini-deep fryer by heating a 4–6-quart pot on a high flame, adding 6 cups corn oil and heating to 350°. Drop okra into pot, 2 cups at a time. Fry to a nice golden brown (approximately 3-4 minutes). Place a paper towel on a plate. When okra is done, scoop out of the oil with a slotted spoon and set it on a plate. Blot with another paper towel.

MUSTARD DIPPING SAUCE Add to a bowl: ½ cup Creole mustard, ½ tablespoon Seasoning Mix #2, 3 tablespoons Worcestershire, 1 teaspoon sugar and ⅛ cup orange juice. Mix together with a whip. Serve at room temperature.

SERVE Place hot fried okra on a plate with mustard dipping sauce on the side.

Serves 4.

OYSTERS BIENVILLE & ROCKEFELLER

There is nothing sexier or more decadent in Hell's Kitchen.

TO PREPARE

(Note: Ingredients should be prepped ahead of time so as not to interrupt sauces.)

PREPARE ROUX   Heat a 1-quart saucepan on low heat. Add ¼ pound butter. Melt very very slowly. Stir in 1 cup flour. *(Note: any leftover roux not used in recipe may be set aside in a cup, set in refrigerator and used later for soups, etc.)*

PREP / COOK ROCKEFELLER   Take 3 bunches fresh spinach. Remove the stems and wash (should make 6 cups). Place in a bowl. Set aside.

Heat a 4-quart pot on medium heat. Add 2 tablespoons margarine and melt. When melted, add ½ cup medium diced onions, 1 cup medium diced green bell pepper, 1 cup medium diced celery, 1 tablespoon fresh chopped garlic and 2 tablespoons Seasoning Mix #2 *(see page 32)*. Stir and simmer for 15 minutes. Next, stir in 1 cup chicken stock. Then add spinach and continue stirring and simmering until it is cooked down (approximately 5 minutes). Add 1 tablespoon roux and 2 tablespoons Pernod liqueur. Stir well.

Next, spoon all ingredients into a food processor and grind completely until smooth. Spoon onto a plate and set in refrigerator for one hour.

PREP / COOK BIENVILLE   Heat a 4-quart pot on medium heat. Add 2 tablespoons margarine. Melt completely. When melted, add 1 cup medium diced onions, ½ cup medium diced green bell pepper, ½ cup medium diced celery, 2 tablespoons Seasoning Mix #2 and 1 tablespoon fresh chopped garlic. Stir and cook for 15 minutes.

Heat an 8-10" skillet on a medium flame. When skillet is hot, add ¼ pound bacon. Render until golden brown and crispy. Add bacon and fat to simmering vegetable mixture. Cook for 2 minutes. Then, stir in 1 cup chicken stock. Next, add ½ cup bay scallops (approximately 4 ounces).

EQUIPMENT LIST

measuring cups and spoons
chopping knife
oyster knife
4-quart pot
8-10" non-stick skillet
2 plates
sheet pan

INGREDIENTS

¼ pound butter
1 cup flour
3 bunches fresh spinach
4 tablespoons margarine
1½ cup medium diced onions
1½ cup medium diced green bell pepper
1½ cup medium diced celery
2 tablespoons fresh chopped garlic
2 tablespoons Seasoning Mix #2
1 cup chicken stock
2 tablespoons Pernod liqueur
2 tablespoons Seasoning Mix #2
¼ pound chopped bacon
1 cup chicken stock
½ cup bay scallops (approximately 4 ounces)
8 (16-20 count) cleaned, de-veined shrimp
1 cup sliced shiitake mushrooms
½ cup chopped scallions
2 tablespoons heavy cream
2 dozen raw oysters

Continued on page 64

OYSTERS BIENVILLE & ROCKEFELLER

(continued)

Take 8 (16-20 count) cleaned, de-veined shrimp. Slice each shrimp into 3 pieces and add to pot along with 1 cup sliced shiitake mushrooms. Bring pot to a boil. Once it comes to a boil, reduce heat to medium and simmer for 4-5 minutes. Then add 4 tablespoons roux. Once sauce begins to thicken after another minute or two, add ½ cup chopped scallions and 2 tablespoons heavy cream. Cook 1 more minute. Remove from heat. Scoop mixture onto a plate. Set plate in refrigerator.

OYSTERS   Take 2 dozen raw oysters. Wash thoroughly using a scrub brush. Pry open back of each shell with an oyster knife. Once open, take knife and gently push underneath each oyster to release it from its shell.

Preheat oven to 350°. Take both plates from refrigerator. Stuff each oyster (1 dozen with Rockefeller, 1 dozen with Bienville, 1 tablespoon each). Place oysters on a sheet pan and put in oven. Cook for 15 minutes.

SERVE   Remove oysters from oven and serve immediately. *Serves 2-4.*

SERVING SUGGESTION   Serve with bowl of Hollandaise Sauce on the side. (See directions for Hollandaise under *Stuffed Mirliton* recipe on page 57).

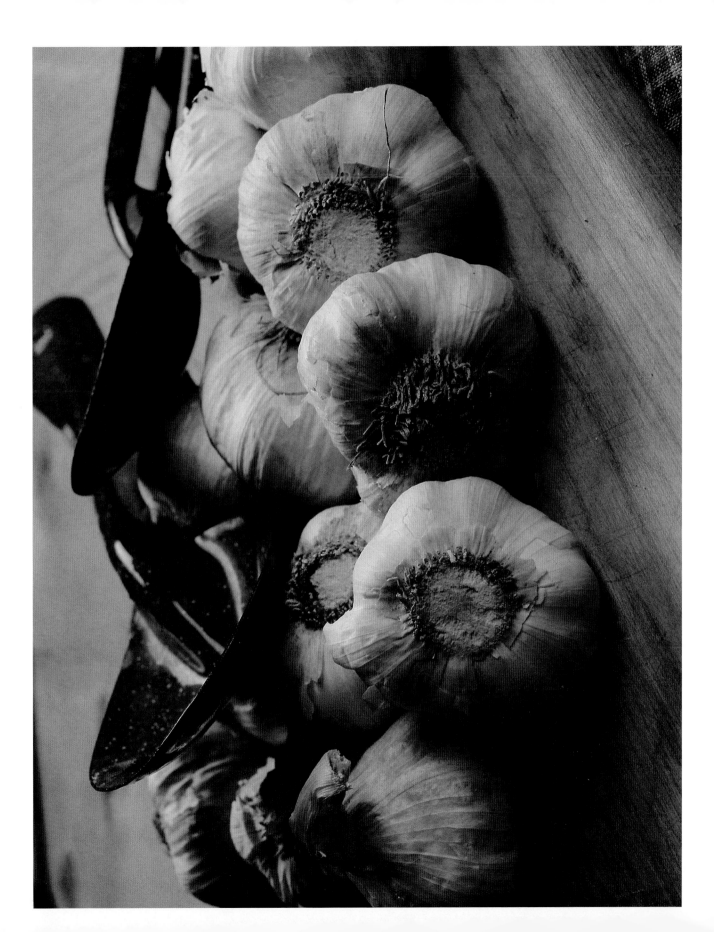

ACORN SQUASH SOUP

EQUIPMENT LIST

measuring cups and spoons
chopping knife
cutting board
large soup spoon
bowl
6-quart pot (short and wide)
hand-held mixer or food processor
whip
ladle (optional)
4 serving bowls

INGREDIENTS

4 acorn squash
2 tablespoons margarine
2 cups medium diced onions
1 cup medium diced green bell pepper
2 cups medium diced celery
1 tablespoon fresh chopped garlic
2 tablespoons Seasoning Mix #2
4 cups chicken stock
½ cup heavy cream

This starter looks great. And tastes even better. Good looking comfort food.

TO PREPARE

SCOOP SQUASH Take 4 acorn squash. Carefully cut off the tops and bottoms. Cut one inch from the top, clean through. Then, take special care when cutting the bottom: only trim enough so squash can "stand" upright and be used as a bowl. Do not cut into squash and create a hole in the bottom. Otherwise, the bowl will leak!

Remove the seeds by scooping them out with a large soup spoon. (Discard seeds and rinse squash.) Then, using the spoon (and a knife for sides), remove all but ¼" of the squash meat by carving around the inside of each squash without cutting into shell. Place meat into a bowl and set aside. Place squash and their tops in refrigerator.

PREP VEGGIES Heat a 6-quart pot on a medium flame. Melt 2 tablespoons margarine then stir in 2 cups medium diced onions, 1 cup medium diced green bell pepper, 2 cups medium diced celery, and 1 tablespoon fresh chopped garlic. Mix together, then add 2 tablespoons Seasoning Mix #2 (*see page 32*). Continue to sauté, approximately 10 minutes. Keep an eye on vegetables, repeating a "stick and scrape" (let it cook, stick, then scrape the bottom and stir back into the vegetable mixture) as you go.

After 10 minutes, stir in squash meat to mixture. Next, add 4 cups chicken stock and bring to a boil. After pot reaches boiling point, reduce flame back to medium. Let simmer until squash gets soft (approximately 8–10 minutes).

BLEND Either use a hand-held mixer to blend ingredients while still in the pot or pour mixture into a food processor. Grind until smooth, then pour back into pot.

SIMMER SOUP Preheat oven to 350°. Return pot to a simmer. Add ½ cup heavy cream and whip into the soup for 3 minutes. Remove pot from heat. Take acorn bowls out of refrigerator. Place on sheet pan with small amount of water. Place in oven for 5 minutes. Remove and place in serving bowls (just in case they leak!) Ladle soup into bowls and serve. *Serves 4.*

ROASTED ANDOUILLE AND BLACK BEAN CHICKEN SOUP

This combination of hearty chicken and black beans with spicy andouille is perfect for a wind-whipping New York City winter night.

TO PREPARE

(Note: Black beans should be soaked overnight before preparing soup. Place beans in container, cover with twice as much water and place in refrigerator.)

ANDOUILLE   Preheat oven to 350°. Take ½ pound andouille. Cut it lengthwise, then cut both pieces lengthwise again, making 4 pieces. Dice these long strips into ¼" pieces (makes 2 cups). Place on roasting pan. Put in oven and roast until andouille is golden brown (approximately 10-15 minutes).

COOK VEGGIES   While andouille is roasting, heat a 6-quart pot over a medium flame. Add 3 tablespoons margarine and melt. When melted, add 3 cups medium diced onions, 2 cups medium diced green bell pepper, 1 cup medium diced celery, 1 tablespoon fresh chopped garlic, and 3 tablespoons Seasoning Mix #1 *(see page 32)*. Stir and cook for approximately 10 minutes.

When veggies begin to get soft, add 1 pound black beans, 1 tablespoon chili powder, 1 tablespoon cumin and ¼ cup fresh chopped cilantro. Continue cooking (approximately 20 minutes). Stir occasionally.

SIMMER   After 20 minutes, add 8 cups chicken stock to the veggie mixture. Stir and cook an additional 20 minutes, until beans are soft and chewy. (Test one by biting into it. If it's hard, go longer. If it's soft . . . done.)

When done, take ¼ mixture and put in food processor. Pulse 5-6 times, breaking up mixture until it's just a bit smooth. Scoop back into pot. Then add the roasted andouille and 2 cups diced chicken breasts (uncooked). Stir and continue simmering for 15 minutes. *(Note: Consistency will be half-way between soup and chili. If mixture becomes too thick, add 1 additional cup chicken stock.)*

SERVE   Ladle into bowls and top with chopped scallions and 1 dollop sour cream. Garnish with chips. *Serves 6-8.*

EQUIPMENT LIST

measuring cups and spoons
chopping knife
cutting board
6-quart pot
food processor
roasting pan
ladle

INGREDIENTS

1 pound black beans (soaked overnight)
½ pound andouille (Cajun smoked pork sausage) *(note: may substitute chorizo)*
3 tablespoons margarine
3 cups medium diced onions
2 cups medium diced green bell pepper
1 cup medium diced celery
1 tablespoon fresh chopped garlic
3 tablespoons Seasoning Mix #1
1 tablespoon chili powder
1 tablespoon cumin
¼ cup fresh chopped cilantro
8-9 cups chicken stock
2 cups diced chicken breasts (uncooked)
6-8 teaspoons chopped scallions
6-8 dollops sour cream

CRAWFISH BISQUE

A little bit sauce. A little bit soup. Here's a cajun twist on an elegant appetizer starring everyone's favorite N'awlins shellfish.

EQUIPMENT LIST

measuring cups and spoons
chopping knife
cutting board
8-10" skillet (at least 2" deep)
4-6-quart pot
fine strainer
whip
large spoon

INGREDIENTS

4 cups medium diced onions
3 cups medium diced green bell pepper
2 cups medium diced celery
2 cups corn oil
2½ cups flour
1 tablespoon Seasoning Mix #1
2 tablespoons Worcestershire sauce
1 tablespoon fresh chopped garlic
2 tablespoons Seasoning Mix #2
½ pound crawfish tailmeat
4 cups chicken stock
1 cup heavy cream
1 teaspoon salt
1 teaspoon corn starch
2 teaspoons water
2 tablespoons Pernod liqueur

TO PREPARE

PREPARE DARK ROUX (*Note: Preparing roux is kind of intense—the oil gets hot and bubbly and everything moves quickly. Don't be intimidated! Hang in there.*) Chop 1 cup medium diced onions, 1 cup medium diced green bell pepper and 1 cup medium diced celery. Set aside.

Heat 2 cups corn oil in an 8-10" skillet (at least 2" deep) over a high flame until it begins to smoke. When smoke appears, slowly add 2½ cups flour, using a whip to stir as you go. Don't stop stirring! Flour will turn a dark, rich brown after 10-15 minutes. Remove skillet from heat and stir in vegetables (above), 1 tablespoon Seasoning Mix #1 (*see page 32*) and 2 tablespoons Worcestershire sauce.

SAUTÉ VEGGIES Heat a 4-6-quart pot on medium heat. Add 3 cups medium diced onions, 2 cups medium diced green bell pepper, 1 cup medium diced celery, and 1 tablespoon fresh chopped garlic. Sauté for 10 minutes. Then add 2 tablespoons Seasoning Mix #2 (*see page 32*) and continue to sauté an additional 20 minutes.

ADD CRAWFISH After 30 minutes, add ½ pound crawfish tailmeat and 4 cups chicken stock. (*Note: Since crawfish already has a seafood taste, Greg prefers chicken over seafood stock to even out the flavor. It makes the sauce more subtle — no overkill.*) Cook an additional 15 minutes. Then add ½ cup dark roux (see above).

STRAIN Take a fine strainer and place it over a bowl. Pour the contents of the pot through the strainer to separate veggies and crawfish from the liquid. Then, pour the liquid back into the pot.

Take the veggies and crawfish, empty them into a food processor and grind them up by pulsing several times. Then, return the mixture to the pot which should be on a medium flame.

Next, stir in 1 cup heavy cream and 1 teaspoon salt to pot. Take a coffee cup and stir together 1 teaspoon corn starch and 2 teaspoons water. Add to pot. Continue to simmer. Just before serving add 2 tablespoons Pernod liqueur. *Serves 4-6*

Talk about comfort food. Jambalaya is your grandmother, your teddy bear and a hot toddy all stirred into one rib-sticking dish. There are many different recipes for this Cajun classic. The secret to this sweat-inducing version is the Cajun specialties: tasso and andouille.

Feel free to add or take away and make your own jumble. That's what makes Jambalaya . . . Jambalaya.

TO PREPARE

STICK AND SCRAPE   Heat an 8-quart pot on a medium flame. Add 3 tablespoons margarine. Melt completely. Add 2 cups tasso and cook on a ¾ high flame. This is a very important stage: the goal is to get the tasso brown. The seasoning will come off the tasso and be returned to the mixture by repeating a "stick and scrape" (let it cook, stick, then scrape the bottom and stir back in). Continue to "stick and scrape" for approximately 15 minutes. *(Note: If tasso begins to get too sticky, remove from flame for a few seconds, wait for sticking, scrape, stir and return to flame.)*

At 8-minute mark, add 4 cups onions, 3 cups bell pepper, and 2 cups celery (all medium diced). Also add 2 tablespoons fresh chopped garlic. Smother vegetables together with the tasso.

ANDOUILLE   Preheat oven to 350°. Take 1 pound andouille and cut it in half lengthwise. Slice those two pieces into ½-inch circles, then cut those circles in half again. Place andouille on sheet pan, put in oven and roast to a nice light brown (approximately 15 minutes).

BACK TO TASSO AND VEGGIES   Mixture has been cooking approximately 20 minutes. Stir in 3 tablespoons finely diced fresh jalapeño and 2 tablespoons Seasoning Mix #1 *(see page 32)*. Stir every 2 minutes or so. Repeat "stick and scrape" when necessary. Remove andouille from oven *(if after 15 minutes it looks light brown)* and add it to the mixture. The juice too! Continue to cook *(so far, the mixture has been cooking about 25 minutes)*. "Stick and scrape" another couple of times. Then add 1 cup chicken stock to deglaze the bottom of the pot. Finally, stir in one 28-ounce can crushed tomatoes.

Mixture has been cooking for approximately 30 minutes. Continue cooking another 30 minutes until texture is nice and stewy. (Total cooking time so far: 1 hour.) Stir in 1 pound diced chicken and cook an additional 15 minutes. *(Note: chicken may be substituted with seafood, tender beef, veal or pork.)*

Add 4 cups cooked white rice and 1 cup chopped green onions. Mix together and serve hot. *Serves 6–8. (Note: Jambalaya may be prepared ahead of time and refrigerated. Do not add rice until warm and ready to serve.)*

EQUIPMENT LIST

measuring cups and spoons
chopping knife
cutting board
large spoon
8-quart pot

INGREDIENTS

3 tablespoons margarine
2 cups tasso (Cajun pickled pork)
4 cups medium diced onions
3 cups medium diced green bell pepper
2 cups medium diced celery
2 tablespoons fresh chopped garlic
1 pound andouille (Cajun smoked pork sausage)
3 tablespoons finely diced fresh jalapeño
2 tablespoons Seasoning Mix #1
1 cup chicken stock
one 28-ounce can crushed tomatoes
1 pound diced chicken (uncooked)
4 cups white rice (cooked)
1 cup chopped green onions

DUCK LADY SALAD WITH RASPBERRY SAUCE

This light and lovely dish is named for a famous and eccentric New Orleans resident, "Ruthie, the Duck Lady." Often seen strolling through the French Quarter carrying a bag of live ducks, Ruthie has been the subject of a documentary, was featured in a 1999 Mardi Gras parade and is the namesake of one of the Delta Grill's best-selling dishes.

EQUIPMENT LIST

measuring cups and spoons
chopping knife
cutting board
boning knife
2-quart pot
slotted spoon
tenderizer or meat mallet
empty ketchup bottle
food processor

INGREDIENTS

12-15 ounce duck breast (2 lobes)
1½ tablespoon Seasoning Mix #1
1 teaspoon ground black pepper
2 cups fresh raspberries
½ tablespoon fresh chopped garlic
1 tablespoon sugar
½ tablespoon Creole mustard
2 tablespoons Worcestershire
½ cup balsamic vinegar
2 tablespoons olive oil
¼ cup apple juice
4 cups greens

TO PREPARE

SLICE BREAST   Take a boning knife and gently remove the skin from the duck breast. Be careful not to damage the meat. Cut the skin into strips, then cut again in the opposite direction to make small squares.

COOK CRACKLINS   Take a 2-quart pot and heat on a very low flame. Add the skin to the pot and render them until they turn into a cracklin (a crispy piece of skin or fat, like a cajun crouton). Cook until cracklins are golden brown and crispy (approximately 30 minutes). Check and stir them every few minutes. When done, use a slotted spoon to remove cracklins from pot. Set them on a paper towel. (*Note: 1 tablespoon cracklin fat should be saved to cook duck breasts.*)

SEASON BREAST   Place duck breasts on cutting board. Take a tenderizer or meat mallet and gently pound the breasts just enough to break the tendons in the meat. (*Goal: to keep breast from shrinking while cooking.*) Then, take 1 tablespoon Seasoning Mix #1 (*see page 32*) and sprinkle evenly over duck breasts. Follow with 1 teaspoon ground black pepper.

COOK DUCK BREASTS   Heat an 8-10" non-stick skillet on a medium flame. Add 1 tablespoon cracklin fat to skillet. When hot, place duck breasts in skillet and cook to medium rare for 4-5 minutes on each side. (*Note: If skillet gets too hot and smoky, just pull off the heat for a few seconds and lower the flame.*)

RASPBERRY SAUCE   Add the following to a bowl: 2 cups fresh raspberries, ½ tablespoon fresh chopped garlic, ½ tablespoon Seasoning Mix #1, 1 tablespoon sugar, ½ tablespoon Creole mustard, 2 tablespoons Worcestershire, ½ cup balsamic vinegar, 2 tablespoons olive oil and ¼ cup apple juice. Pour into food processor and grind until smooth.

PREP PLATE   Fill half a plate with your favorite fresh greens. Then, add raspberry sauce. Feeling fancy? Pour raspberry sauce into an empty ketchup bottle and squeeze out onto plate in a gourmet squiggle (or serve on the side). Take cooked duck breast and slice thinly on a diagonal cut. Fan out pieces and arrange on plate over raspberry sauce. Top with cracklins. *Serves 2.*

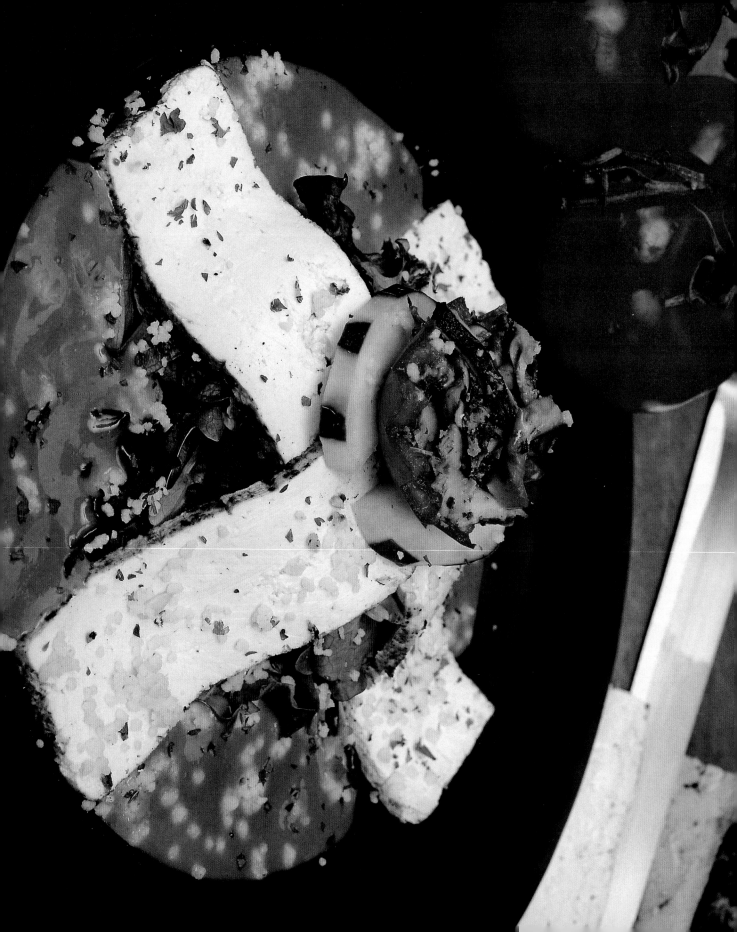

BLACKENED TOFU SALAD

EQUIPMENT LIST

measuring cups and spoons
chopping knife
cutting board
large spoon
spatula
cast iron skillet (or an 8-10" non-stick skillet)
small saucepan
fine strainer
bowl

INGREDIENTS

1 tablespoon + 1 teaspoon Seasoning Mix #2
1 block of tofu (6-8 ounces)
1 tablespoon butter
1 box cous-cous
1 teaspoon fresh chopped garlic
1 cup sliced shiitake mushrooms

Delta Grill patrons clamored for a vegetarian dish. This is what Greg gave them. Hey, meat and potatoes guys! We dare ya!

TO PREPARE

TOFU Sprinkle 1 tablespoon Seasoning Mix #2 (*see page* 32) evenly over 1 block of tofu (6-8 ounces). Heat a cast iron skillet on a high flame (or an 8-10" non-stick skillet over a medium flame). On another burner, heat a small saucepan and melt 1 tablespoon butter. Pour the butter over the tofu and place into skillet. Blacken all sides of block until golden brown and crispy on the outside. Using a spatula, start with tofu facing down, flip it over, then do the sides (approximately 4-5 minutes to blacken the entire block).

COUS-COUS Fill 1-quart saucepan with water and bring to a boil. Empty in 1 box cous-cous (6-8 ounces). Cook until tender (approximately 3 minutes). Be careful not to overcook! Take a fine strainer, hold it over the sink and pour in cous-cous. Rinse with cold water. Scoop into a bowl and set aside.

SAUTÉ MUSHROOMS Heat an 8-10" non-stick skillet. Add 1 teaspoon butter and melt. Next add 1 teaspoon Seasoning Mix #2 and 1 teaspoon fresh chopped garlic. Let cook together for 1 minute. Then add 1 cup sliced shiitake mushrooms. Sauté slowly until tender. When cooked, place on plate and set aside.

PREP PLATE Take 2-4 cups of your favorite greens and arrange them on plates. Take tofu and slice into ¼" slices. Arrange tofu on top of greens. Crumble cous-cous on top, followed by a dollop of shiitake mushrooms. Pour on your favorite dressing. *Serves 2-4.*

STUFFED PINEAPPLE

EQUIPMENT LIST

measuring cups and spoons
chopping knife
cutting board
grapefruit knife (optional)
large spoon
mixing bowl
wok or large skillet
wooden spatula
coffee cup

INGREDIENTS

1 pineapple
1 cup large diced red bell peppers
1 cup zucchini (¼" slices)
1 cup yellow squash (¼" slices)
1 cup carrots (cut diagonally, ¼" slices)
1 cup broccoli florets
1 cup bok choy
¼ cup thinly sliced ginger
3 tablespoons roasted sesame oil
½ tablespoon fresh chopped garlic
1 tablespoon Seasoning Mix #1
2 tablespoons Worcestershire sauce
3 tablespoons hoisin sauce
1 tablespoon soy sauce
½ cup apple juice
1 tablespoon corn starch
3 tablespoons water

The Delta Grill does a brisk lunch business. At lunchtime, people often want something lighter than the usual dinner fare. And sometimes, they want vegetarian. But they want it flavorful. They're New Yorkers; they want it all and aren't afraid to ask for it.

That's how this dish came to be. Is there a Cajun word for Aloha? In New York they say, "hello and goodbye."

TO PREPARE

PINEAPPLE   Get a good, fresh, firm pineapple and slice it in half lengthwise. (So 2 pieces will each have a spiny green top.) Make a tiny flat cut in the bottom so pineapple can stand up without rolling to either side. Take a grapefruit knife (or regular knife) and scoop out inside of pineapple halves, leaving the shells intact to make two pineapple bowls. Remove the core and dice the useable part of the pineapple into bite size chunks.

PREPARE VEGGIES   Add the pineapple and the following to a mixing bowl: 1 cup large diced red bell peppers, 1 cup zucchini (cut diagonally, ¼" slices), 1 cup yellow squash (cut diagonally, ¼" slices), 1 cup carrots (cut diagonally, ¼" slices), 1 cup broccoli florets, and 1 cup bok choy. Mix all ingredients together.

COOK   Prepare ¼ cup thinly sliced ginger. Set to the side.

Take a wok, or a very large skillet and heat on a high flame. Add 3 tablespoons roasted sesame oil. When heated, add ½ tablespoon fresh chopped garlic and the sliced ginger and sauté for approximately 1 minute. Then, add remaining vegetables from bowl and stir for 3 minutes. Next, add 1 tablespoon Seasoning Mix #1 (*see page 32*), 2 tablespoons Worcestershire sauce, 3 tablespoons hoisin sauce, 1 tablespoon soy sauce and ½ cup apple juice.

Take a coffee cup, add 1 tablespoon corn starch, 3 tablespoons water and stir together. Add this to the mixture. Continue to cook for 2 more minutes. Remove vegetables from heat.

SERVE   Take pineapple bowls, place them on plates and fill them with the veggie mixture. *Serves 2.*

BBQ ST. LOUIS RIBS WITH SWEET POTATO STEAK FRIES

This dish is dedicated to Andrew Humbert. With these finger-licking ribs, the secret is in the sauce. Sorry, Greg. It ain't a secret anymore.

TO PREPARE

SEASON RIBS   The night before cooking, take 2 racks of St. Louis ribs and season all sides using 6 tablespoons Seasoning Mix #1 (*see page 32*). Rub seasoning into the meat. Place on a sheet pan and put in refrigerator.

COOK RIBS   Preheat oven to 500º. Take ribs from refrigerator and cook until they "brown off" (approximately 30 minutes).

BBQ SAUCE   Heat a 6-quart pot on a medium flame.   Add 3 tablespoons margarine and melt completely. Add 3 cups small diced onions. Caramelize until golden brown (approximately 20 minutes).

CHECK RIBS   After 30 minutes, remove ribs from oven. Add 1½ cups chicken stock to sheet pan, then completely cover it with aluminum foil, tightly. Reduce oven temperature to 300º and return ribs to oven to slow cook for an additional 1 hour.

BACK TO SAUCE   Add 4 cups ketchup to the still cooking onions. (*Note: 16 ounces to a cup. If using bottles of ketchup, add a little bit of water to get out all the ketchup.*) Add ½ cup honey, ½ cup dark molasses, 1 tablespoon ground black pepper, 2 tablespoons Seasoning Mix #1, ¼ cup Worcestershire, the juice of 1 lemon, 1 tablespoon fresh chopped garlic and 1 cup roasted pecans. (*Note: to roast pecans, stick them in a 400º oven on a sheet pan for 10 minutes.*) Let ingredients simmer together for 1 hour. Then, pour ingredients into food processor, blend, then return to pot. (*Note: use a rubber spatula to get every bit of sauce.*) Simmer an additional 10 minutes.

REMOVE RIBS   Remove ribs from oven. (*Be careful to handle pan evenly to prevent spilling sauce and getting burned.*) Take a large spoon or ladle and scoop some rib drippings, approximately 2 cups, into BBQ sauce. Do not attempt to use all the drippings.

Continued on page 82

EQUIPMENT LIST

measuring cups and spoons
chopping knife
cutting board
sheet pan (approximately 17" x 13" x 1")
sheet pan or cookie sheet (for fries)
two 6-quart pots (short and wide)
aluminum foil
rubber spatula
ladle (optional)
large spoon
baster
candy or oil thermometer

INGREDIENTS

2 racks St. Louis ribs
10 tablespoons Seasoning Mix #1
3 tablespoons margarine
3 cups small diced onions
1½ cups chicken stock
4 cups ketchup
½ cup honey
½ cup dark molasses
1 tablespoon ground black pepper
¼ cup Worcestershire
the juice of 1 lemon
1 tablespoon fresh chopped garlic
1 cup roasted pecans
4 yams
6 cups corn oil

BBQ ST. LOUIS RIBS WITH SWEET POTATO STEAK FRIES

(continued)

STEAK FRIES Pre-heat oven to 350°. Take 4 yams. Cut into steak fries by cutting each one in half, then cutting those halves into quarters. (*Note: extra large yams may be cut into eighths.*) Heat an 8-10″ skillet on a medium flame. Add 2 cups oil. Place pieces in oil and fry until golden brown. Remove and place on sheet pan and bake for 15 minutes. Remove from oven. Sprinkle 2 tablespoons Seasoning Mix #1 (or salt) lightly over fries.

SERVE Break racks in half and place on dinner plates. Ladle sauce over ribs. Serve fries on the side. *Serves 4.* (*Note: Ribs may be cooked ahead of time, even the day before, and heated later on an outdoor grill. Grill first, get ribs hot, then add the sauce just before done. If a sugar-based sauce is added too early, it will caramelize and turn black.*)

NEW YORK STRIP WITH GARLIC BUTTER SAUCE AND MASHED NEW POTATOES

EQUIPMENT LIST

measuring cups and spoons
chopping knife
large spoon
6–8-quart pot
potato masher
broiler pan
1-quart sauce pan
8-10" non-stick skillet
whip
coffee cup

INGREDIENTS

15 red new potatoes
3½ tablespoons butter
½ cup chicken stock
½ cup heavy cream
1 tablespoon + 1 teaspoon Seasoning Mix #1
3 tablespoons fresh chopped garlic
2 teaspoons salt
1 teaspoon ground white pepper
½ cup chopped scallions
two 16-ounce New York Strip steaks
2 tablespoons Seasoning Mix #2
2 tablespoons olive oil
1 tablespoon Worcestershire sauce
1 cup beef stock
2 tablespoons fresh chopped parsley
1 tablespoon corn starch
2 tablespoons water
¼ teaspoon salt

New York is actually a city made up of dozens and dozens of neighborhoods. New Yorkers get to have their own small towns by visiting their regular deli guy, baker and, of course, butcher. Visit your butcher and ask him for the best aged and slightly marbleized cut of New York Strip he's got. And, hey Mack! Call him by name, will ya?

TO PREPARE

NEW POTATOES   Take 15 red new potatoes and cut into quarters. (*Note: do not remove the skins.*) Place them in a 6–8-quart pot. Cover potatoes completely with water and place on a high flame. Bring to a boil. Continue boiling, approximately 25 minutes, until potatoes are fork tender. Strain the water off, then return potatoes to same pot. Add the following to the potatoes: 2 tablespoons butter, ½ cup chicken stock, ½ cup heavy cream, 1 tablespoon Seasoning Mix #1 (*see page 32*), 2 tablespoons fresh chopped garlic, 2 teaspoons salt, and 1 teaspoon ground white pepper. Mash all ingredients together with the potatoes. (*Note: mixture should not be mashed smooth; leave it a little chunky.*) Then stir in ½ cup chopped scallions. Keep warm until serving.

NEW YORK STRIP   Preheat oven to 400°. Take two 16-ounce New York Strip steaks. Season steaks evenly, on both sides, with 2 tablespoons Seasoning Mix # 1. Heat an 8-10" non-stick skillet on a medium flame. Add ½ tablespoon butter, spreading evenly in skillet. When butter begins to brown, add steaks and cook for 2 minutes on each side. Goal: a nice, caramelized brown color. Remove steaks from skillet, place on broiler pan and cook in oven until done according to taste (rare, medium or well-done). Example: medium rare (135° internal temperature) takes 9-10 minutes. While steaks are cooking, prepare sauce.

GARLIC BUTTER SAUCE   Heat 2 tablespoons olive oil on medium heat in a 1-quart sauce pan. When oil begins to smoke, add 1 tablespoon fresh chopped garlic. It will turn white almost immediately. When it begins to get brown, after about 1 minute, quickly add 1 teaspoon Seasoning Mix #1 and 1 tablespoon Worcestershire sauce. Next add 1 cup beef stock. (*Note: Continue cooking on medium heat throughout.*) Return mixture to a boil. Let it simmer for 2 minutes, then add 1 tablespoon butter. Whip vigorously. Stir in 2 tablespoons fresh chopped parsley. Take a coffee cup, add 1 tablespoon corn starch and 2 tablespoons water. Stir together, then add to the sauce.

SERVE   When steaks are finished, remove from oven. Slice into thin strips or serve whole. Scoop sauce onto dinner plates with a ladle or a spoon. Place steak strips on top of sauce. Serve with potatoes on the side. *Serves 2.*

BLACKENED LAMB CHOPS WITH MANGO-MINT SALSA

To most Americans, Cajun means "blackened." Try this recipe to find out blackened means flavorful not burnt. The lamb chops are cooled on top with a refreshing salsa.

TO PREPARE

Mango-Mint Salsa: Part 1

MINT   Take bowl #1 (minimum size: 1 quart) and the mint leaves. Pick 3 tablespoons of mint leaves from the stems, placing the leaves in the bowl. When finished, fill the bowl halfway with water. Massage leaves to release any dirt. Set bowl aside for 15 minutes. Leaves will rise to the top, dirt will settle to bottom.

PREP TOMATO   While leaves are soaking, take saucepan, fill halfway with water and bring to a boil. Take the tomato and score it. (Make an x-mark on the bottom of it with a knife.) Then, using a tomato shark or knife, remove the core from the top and place tomato (minus core) into the boiling water for about 30 seconds. When the skin begins to come loose, use tongs to remove the tomato from the water. Gently peel off the skin and discard it. Put tomato on a plate and set in refrigerator to cool for 5 minutes. When tomato is cooled, take it out, chop into finely diced chunks and place in bowl #2.

PREP VEGGIES   Finely dice ½ cup celery, ½ cup onions, ½ cup yellow bell pepper and ½ cup green bell pepper and add it to bowl #2.

PREP MANGO   Peel the mango and discard skin. Remove the meat from the pit, finely dice it and add to bowl #2.

ADDITIONAL INGREDIENTS   Mix into bowl #2: 2 tablespoons Seasoning Mix #1 *(see page 32)*, the juice of 1 lime, and 1½ cups tomato juice.

Then, remove the mint leaves from bowl #1 very gently, using your finger tips. Be careful not to disturb the water and bring the dirt back onto the leaves! Chop leaves into finely diced pieces. Then, add the leaves to bowl #2 and set salsa aside at room temperature.

EQUIPMENT LIST

measuring cups and spoons
chopping knife
cutting board
2 bowls (one, 1 quart or larger)
peeler
1-quart saucepan
tomato shark (optional)
tongs
plate
plastic wrap

INGREDIENTS

3 tablespoons fresh mint, finely chopped
   (approximately 1 bunch)
1 medium tomato, peeled and finely diced
½ cup finely diced celery
½ cup finely diced onions
½ cup finely diced yellow bell pepper
½ cup finely diced green bell pepper
1 ripe mango, peeled and finely diced
2 tablespoons Seasoning Mix #1
juice of 1 lime
1½ cups tomato juice

Continued on page 88

BLACKENED LAMB CHOPS WITH MANGO-MINT SALSA

(continued)

EQUIPMENT LIST

1-quart sauce pan

8-10" cast iron skillet (may substitute with a non-stick skillet)

INGREDIENTS

12 lamb chops (1" thick)

2 tablespoons Seasoning Mix # 1

3 tablespoons butter

TO PREPARE

Lamb Chops: Part 2

SEASON LAMB CHOPS   Take 2 tablespoons Seasoning Mix # 1 and gently rub into both sides of each chop. Place chops on a plate, cover with plastic wrap and set in refrigerator for 1 hour.

MELT BUTTER   Heat a 1-quart saucepan on a low flame. Add 3 tablespoons butter and melt slowly. (Note: see Hollandaise section under "Stuffed Mirliton" recipe, page 57.) The butter should separate into 3 layers.

Remove chops from refrigerator. Take off plastic wrap.

BLACKENING   Take a 8-10" cast iron skillet and heat on a medium flame. IMPORTANT: skillet must be hot before meat is added for proper blackening.

Place one teaspoonful of just the butter fat (the middle layer of the melted butter) on top of each chop. Add 4 chops at a time to the heated skillet and cook for 3-4 minutes on each side for medium rare chops. One teaspoon of butter plus the meat's own fat will be plenty to cook them. (Note: To make well-done chops, cook on each side for 4 minutes, then place them on a sheet pan into an oven pre-heated to 400°). Do not cook longer than 4 minutes on each side or they will burn. Serves 4 (3 chops each).

SUGGESTED SIDE DISH   Rice or Jalapeño Mashed Potatoes (see next recipe).

JALAPEÑO MASHED POTATOES

Suggested side dish for blackened lamb chops. When Greg worked at K. Paul's, they always served awesome mashed potatoes. Heavy on the butter and cream. They were great. Add a little jalapeño and cheddar cheese and they become . . . to die for. A melt-in-your-mouth side dish.

EQUIPMENT LIST

measuring cups and spoons
chopping knife
cutting board
4-quart pot
saucepan
fork
strainer
potato masher
spoon
cheese grater
potato masher

INGREDIENTS

5 potatoes (one potato for each person + one for good luck)
¼ pound butter
1 cup heavy cream
1 cup grated sharp cheddar cheese
1 tablespoon fresh chopped jalapeño

TO PREPARE

Peel potatoes, cut each one in half and place them in a pot. Cover them with water and bring pot to a boil. Continue boiling for 25 minutes until they are fork tender (a fork will run directly through them with no force).

While potatoes are cooking, take saucepan and melt together ¼ pound butter and 1 cup heavy cream. Set aside.

Strain potatoes and place them back into the pot used to cook them.

Add 1 cup grated sharp cheddar cheese and 1 tablespoon fresh chopped jalapeño to potatoes.

Take a potato masher, and smoosh the cheese, jalapeño and potatoes together. Go ahead and leave some lumps — the potatoes shouldn't be perfectly smooth. Next, using a spoon, slowly add the butter and cream and combine with potatoes. Serve hot. *Serves 4.*

(Note: If potatoes get cold, add them to a pot, and beat. Add a small amount of cream or chicken stock and stir it in.)

STUFFED PORK CHOPS WITH RICE DRESSING

EQUIPMENT LIST

measuring cups and spoons
chopping knife
small paring knife
cutting board
8-10" skillet
plate
roasting pan
2-quart saucepan
aluminum foil

INGREDIENTS

3 cups medium diced onions
2 cups medium diced green bell pepper
2 cups medium diced celery
2 cups corn oil
2½ cups flour
5 tablespoons Seasoning Mix #1
2 tablespoons Worcestershire sauce
2 tablespoons margarine
2 tablespoons fresh chopped garlic
½ pound ground beef
4¼ cups chicken stock
2 cups cooked rice
½ cup sliced scallions
4 pork chops (1¼" thick)

TO PREPARE

PREPARE DARK ROUX (*Note: preparing roux is kind of intense — the oil gets hot and bubbly and everything moves quickly. Don't be intimidated! Hang in there.*) Chop 1 cup medium diced onions, 1 cup medium diced green bell pepper and 1 cup medium diced celery. Set aside. Heat 2 cups corn oil in an 8-10" skillet (at least 2" deep) over a high flame until it begins to smoke. When smoke appears, slowly add 2½ cups flour, using a whip to stir as you go. Don't stop stirring! Flour will turn a dark, rich brown after 10-15 minutes. Remove skillet from heat and stir in vegetables (above), 1 tablespoon Seasoning Mix #1 and 2 tablespoons Worcestershire sauce. Set aside, but keep warm.

RICE DRESSING Heat an 8-10" skillet on medium flame. Add 2 tablespoons margarine and melt. When melted, add 1 cup medium diced onions, ½ cup medium diced green bell pepper, ½ cup medium diced celery, 1 tablespoon Seasoning Mix #1 (*see page 32*) and 1 tablespoon fresh chopped garlic. Cook for 15-20 minutes. Vegetables will get soft, then begin to caramelize. Repeat a "stick and scrape" (let it cook, stick, then scrape the bottom and stir back into the vegetable mixture) as you go. After 20 minutes, add ½ pound ground beef and mash into the mixture (texture will appear granular). Continue cooking, stirring and mashing the beef, an additional 15-20 minutes. Add ¼ cup chicken stock, 2 cups cooked rice and ½ cup sliced scallions. Stir and cook another 5 minutes. Scoop mixture onto a plate. Place in refrigerator.

PREP / STUFF / SEASON / COOK PORK CHOPS Preheat oven to 350º. Take 4 pork chops (1¼" thick), and use a small paring knife to make a ½" slit in each chop. (Be careful not to make the slit too big.) After making slit, slide knife diagonally into chop to make a small pocket for stuffing later.

Remove dressing from refrigerator. Stuff each chop's pocket with as much dressing as it will hold. Then, take 2 tablespoons Seasoning Mix #1 and season evenly on both sides of each chop. Place into roasting pan. Put pan in oven and cook until chops have browned (approximately 10-15 minutes).

GRAVY Heat a 2-quart saucepan on a medium flame. Add 2 tablespoons margarine and melt. When melted, add 1 cup onions, ½ cup green bell pepper, ½ cup celery, 1 tablespoon fresh chopped garlic and 1 tablespoon Seasoning Mix #1. Sauté until veggies begin to get brown (approximately 15 minutes).

Continued on page 92

STUFFED PORK CHOPS WITH RICE DRESSING

(continued)

After 15 minutes, add almost 4 cups chicken stock to the pot (set 4 tablespoons aside). Bring to a simmer. Once mixture begins simmering, take a separate bowl and add 2 tablespoons dark roux and the 4 tablespoons chicken stock which was set aside. Stir until smooth, then add contents of the bowl to the veggie mixture in the pot.

BACK TO CHOPS Remove chops from oven. Pour gravy over the chops and wrap the roasting pan tightly with aluminum foil. Return pan to oven. Lower oven heat to 300° and cook for an additional 15-20 minutes.

When done, remove chops from oven. Pour gravy from bottom of roasting pan back into the 1-quart sauce pan. If necessary, thicken by mixing 1 tablespoon corn starch and 2 tablespoons water in a coffee cup, then pour into gravy.

SERVE Place pork chops on dinner plates. Pour gravy on top and serve with favorite vegetable. *Serves 4*

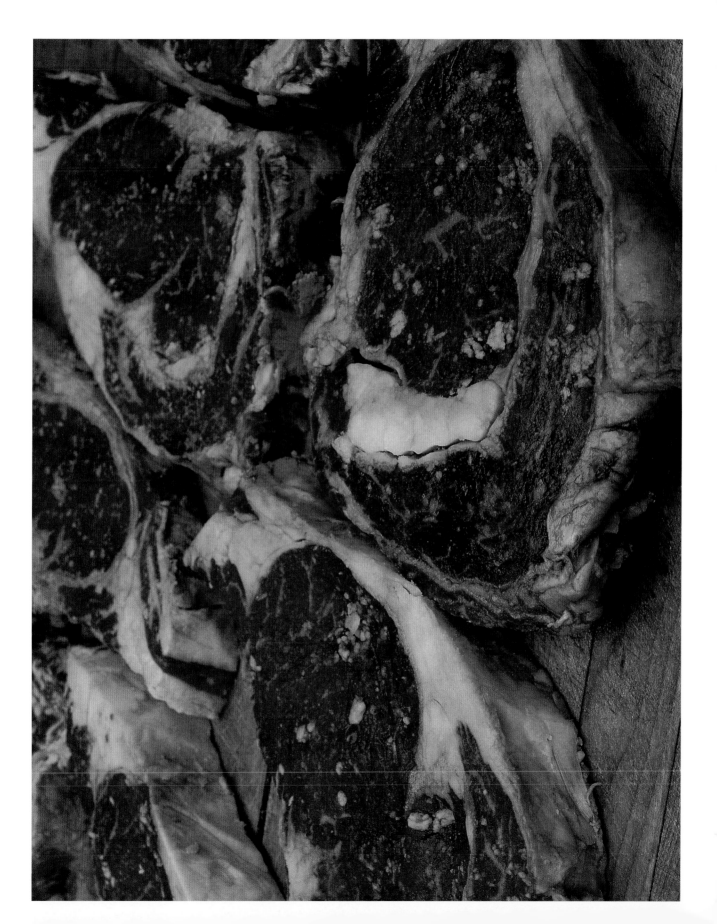

BLUE PLATE SPECIAL — SAUTÉED CHICKEN WITH PORTABELLO MUSHROOMS IN A FRESH TOMATO CREAM SAUCE

Cooks are always looking for a new way to make chicken. This casserole-like recipe is fast. Something to throw together quick. But it is absolutely delicious and just a little exotic with its portabello mushrooms and wild rice.

EQUIPMENT LIST

measuring cups and spoons
chopping knife
cutting board
large spoon
4-quart pot
bowl

INGREDIENTS

1 pound chicken breast
3 tablespoons Seasoning Mix #1
¼ cup olive oil
1 cup small diced onions
1 tablespoon fresh chopped garlic
3 cups large diced portabello mushrooms
2 cups large diced plum tomatoes
1 cup small diced scallions
1 cup chicken stock
½ cup heavy cream
¼ teaspoon salt
wild rice (approximately ½ cup cooked per person)

TO PREPARE

Dice 1 pound chicken breast and place in a bowl. Add 1 tablespoon Seasoning Mix #1 (*see page 32*). Mix thoroughly.

Heat a 4-quart pot. Add ¼ cup olive oil. Add 1 cup small diced onions and 1 tablespoon fresh chopped garlic and cook for two minutes on a medium flame, stirring intermittently. The onions should look clear, and the garlic should start to lightly brown.

Add chicken to onions and garlic mixture. Next add 3 cups large diced portabello mushrooms, 1 tablespoon Seasoning Mix #1, 2 cups large diced plum tomatoes and 1 cup scallions (cut ½ inch off top of green onions, then cut lengthwise from top of green part to the bottom).

Sauté for 2 minutes on medium flame, then add 1 cup chicken stock and ½ cup heavy cream. Add another tablespoon Seasoning Mix #1 and ¼ teaspoon salt. Let simmer 5 minutes. Serve over wild rice. *Serves 2.*

FRIED CHICKEN WITH COLLARD GREENS AND CANDIED YAMS

Colonel, beware. Southern all the way.

TO PREPARE

PREP / BAKE CHICKEN   Preheat oven to 350°. Take a whole, 3½ pound chicken. Cut into 8 pieces (or ask butcher to do it). Place pieces in a large bowl. Add 2 tablespoons Seasoning Mix #2 (*see page 32*), ¼ cup Worcestershire Sauce, and ¼ cup hot sauce (or pepper sauce) into the bowl and rub into chicken. Then place the chicken onto a sheet pan and into the oven. Completely cook chicken (approximately 20-25 minutes). Remove from oven and place into refrigerator to chill.

PREP / COOK COLLARD GREENS   Take 2 bunches collard greens. Clean by removing (and discarding) stems. Cut bunches into 1½" squares. Wash thoroughly. Set aside.

Heat an 8-quart pot on a medium flame. Add 3 tablespoons margarine and melt. When melted add 2 cups onions, 1 cup green bell pepper, 1 cup celery, 1 tablespoon fresh chopped garlic and 2 tablespoons Seasoning Mix #2. Stir and cook for 15 minutes. Then, deglaze the pan by stirring in 3 cups chicken stock. Reduce flame to low. Next, begin slowly adding clean greens. When all greens have been added, stir and cook for an additional 15-20 minutes.

Heat an 8" skillet on a medium flame. When skillet is hot, add ½ pound bacon, (diced into ½" squares). Render until crispy, and golden brown (approximately 15 minutes). When cooked, add the bacon and fat to the simmering collard greens. Continue simmering until greens are tender.

PREP / COOK CANDIED YAMS   Heat a 4-quart pot on a medium flame. Add ½ pound dark brown sugar (packed), ½ pound butter, 2 cups orange juice, ½ tablespoon cinnamon, and ½ tablespoon nutmeg. Stir and cook until melted.

While mixture is simmering, take 3 yams. Peel, cut into ½" strips and wash. Then add strips to the pot and cook until yams are tender (approximately 25 minutes). *Note: Yams should be served hot. Re-heating is not a good idea.*

Continued on page 98

EQUIPMENT LIST

measuring cups and spoons
chopping knife
3 bowls
sheet pan
4–6-quart pot, 8-quart pot
8" skillet
food processor
candy or oil thermometer

INGREDIENTS

whole, 3½-pound chicken
6 tablespoons Seasoning Mix #2
¼ cup Worcestershire Sauce
¼ cup hot sauce or pepper sauce
2 bunches collard greens
3 tablespoons margarine
2 cups medium diced onions
1 cup medium diced green bell pepper
1 cup medium diced celery
1 tablespoon fresh chopped garlic
3 cups chicken stock
½ pound bacon (diced into ½" squares)
1 package corn tortilla chips
4 cups flour
3 eggs
2 cups milk
6 cups corn oil
½ pound dark brown sugar (packed)
½ pound butter
2 cups orange juice
½ tablespoon cinnamon
½ tablespoon nutmeg
3 yams

FRIED CHICKEN WITH COLLARD GREENS AND CANDIED YAMS

(continued)

BACK TO CHICKEN   Take 2 bowls and 1 package corn tortilla chips (chips may be flavored with tomatoes, be creative!) Place a handful of chips in a food processor and pulse several times until they are in small pieces, but not dust. Continue grinding until there are 2 cups ground chips. (*Note: If you don't have a food processor, simply crumble the chips by hand.*) Place chips in bowl #1. Also add 4 cups flour, and 2 tablespoons Seasoning Mix #2. In bowl #2, add 3 eggs and 2 cups milk. Whip together.

Make a mini-deep fryer by heating a 4–6-quart pot on a high flame, adding 6 cups corn oil and heating to 360°. While oil is heating, bread the chicken by dipping each piece first in bowl #1, then bowl #2, then back to bowl #1. When breaded, set each piece on a plate. Repeat for all chicken pieces.

When oil is hot, fry one piece of chicken at a time. Remember, chicken is already cooked. The goal is to get the chicken crispy on the outside and heat it up on the inside. Check temperature continuously. (Temperature may drop when chicken is dropped in oil. Adjust flame, higher and lower, to keep temperature at 360°.) Fry each piece for 4 minutes. Remove with tongs and place on plate covered with paper towel.

SERVE   Serve warm with collard greens and candied yams.

LENORE'S CHICKEN WITH ANDOUILLE STUFFING AND CHEESE HOLLANDAISE

This decadent dish is named for someone, but Greg's not talking.

EQUIPMENT LIST

measuring cups and spoons
chopping knife
large spoon
10" skillet (at least 2" deep)
food processor
bowl
plate
wooden mallet
plastic wrap
3 loaf pans (9¼" x 5½" x 2½") (or may substitute 3 large bowls)
4-quart pot
2 forks
sheet pan

INGREDIENTS

3 tablespoons margarine
3 cups medium diced onions
2 cups medium diced green bell pepper
1 cup medium diced celery
1 tablespoon fresh chopped garlic
1 pound andouille
2 tablespoons Seasoning Mix #1
½ cup chicken stock
½ cup unseasoned bread crumbs
½ cup sliced scallions
four 6-8 oz. sliced chicken breasts
1 cup flour
3 eggs
½ cup milk
unseasoned bread crumbs
1 cup corn oil

TO PREPARE

ANDOUILLE STUFFING   Heat a 10" skillet (at least 2" deep) on a high flame. Add 3 tablespoons margarine. When melted, add 3 cups medium diced onions, 2 cups medium diced green bell pepper, 1 cup medium diced celery and 1 tablespoon freshly chopped garlic. While veggies are cooking, take 1 pound andouille and cut into 1 inch pieces. Then put andouille in a food processor. Grind well, until it reaches a ground beef texture (very small chunks). Place in a bowl. Set aside.

After veggies have cooked for approximately 6 minutes, stir in 2 tablespoons Seasoning Mix #1 (*see page 32*). Lower flame to medium. Add andouille to mixture. Continue stirring and cooking another 20-25 minutes (andouille should appear golden brown). Add ½ cup chicken stock. Cook for 3 minutes, then stir in ½ cup unseasoned bread crumbs. Continue cooking 3 more minutes. Lastly, add ½ cup sliced scallions. (*Optional, but highly recommended. They help cool the palette while adding color to andouille.*) Remove mixture from heat and scoop out onto a plate. Place in refrigerator for 1 hour.

PREP CHICKEN   Cover a cutting board with a sheet of plastic wrap. Take one 6-8 ounce sliced chicken breast and cover with another sheet of plastic wrap. Pound the breast until it becomes a flat "sheet" of chicken, 12" across. Remove top sheet of plastic wrap. Repeat for all 4 pieces.

Remove stuffing from refrigerator. Take ½ cup stuffing and roll it between your hands like a tube. Place "tube" on top of breast sheet. Take the bottom part of breast sheet and fold it over stuffing. Then, take the ends of the breast sheet and fold them in. (Lift bottom sheet of plastic wrap to help roll.) Continue to roll up the rest of the sheet into a cylinder. (It should resemble a burrito.) Repeat until there are four uncooked cylinders or "Lenores." Place on plate. Set aside.

BREADING   First, take 3 loaf pans (9¼" x 5½" x 2½") or substitute with 3 large bowls. To pan #1, add 1 cup flour. To pan #2, add 3 eggs and ½ cup milk. Whip together until frothy. To pan #3, add 2 cups unseasoned bread crumbs. Take each Lenore and bread it by dipping into pan #1, #2 then #3. Cover each Lenore evenly and completely, then place on a plate.

Continued on page 102

LENORE'S CHICKEN WITH ANDOUILLE STUFFING AND CHEESE HOLLANDAISE

(continued)

FRYING   First, preheat oven to 350°. Heat an 8-10" non-stick skillet. Add 1 cup corn oil. When oil is hot, place each Lenore into oil and brown each side until golden brown. Use 2 forks to carefully turn each one while they are frying. (Be careful not to pierce the Lenores or crack them in half.) Then, place fried Lenores on a sheet pan and bake in oven at 350° for 20 minutes.

SAUCE   Please see Hollandaise instructions under *Stuffed Mirliton Recipe* found on page 57. *Note: For this recipe, stir ½ cup grated sharp cheddar cheese into the sauce at the very end.*

SERVING   Remove Lenores from oven. Slice the ends off each Lenore then slice them down the middle. Then make a diagonal cut in the same direction on the two pieces. Coat bottom of plate with cheese Hollandaise. Then place sliced Lenores on plate standing up (flat side on bottom). Serve with a vegetable side dish. *Serves 4.*

CHILEAN SEA BASS WITH AVOCADO PURÉE AND SAUTÉED PLANTAINS

Greg likes Sea Bass because it's always one of the best looking fish at the Fulton Fish Market. It's sweet and has a great, almost fluffy texture. Feel free to substitute your favorite fish. But not for nothing, the Sea Bass can't be beat.

TO PREPARE

PURÉE   Take 3 medium-sized, ripe avocados. Peel them, remove the pits and cut avocado meat into chunks. Place chunks in 2-quart bowl. Also add to bowl: 2 cups medium diced ripe tomatoes, 1 tablespoon fresh chopped garlic, 2 tablespoons Seasoning Mix #1 (*see page 32*), 4 tablespoons Worcestershire sauce, 1 medium diced jalapeño (1 tablespoon), 3 tablespoons fresh cut cilantro, ¼ cup finely diced onions, ¼ cup finely diced red bell pepper, juice from 1 lemon, juice from 1 lime and 1 teaspoon salt. Stir together, then add 1 cup cold chicken stock. Take above mixture and pour it into a food processor. Add ¼ cup cold chicken stock. (*Note: if all the mixture won't fit in the food processor, just blend a little bit at a time.*) Begin to grind. Continue grinding until smooth. Result: approximately 4 cups of sauce (1 cup for each dish).

PREP PLANTAINS   Take 2 green plantains. First, chop off both tops and bottoms. Make a cut just through the skin, lengthwise, from top to bottom. Peel the skin away from the meat. Chop both plantains into ½" pieces. Heat an 8" frying pan on a medium flame. Add 1 cup corn oil. When oil is hot, fry plantains 2 minutes on each side until golden brown. Place on a plate. Take several at a time and place on a cutting board. Cover with plastic wrap. Lightly mash plantains using the bottom of a small plate. Be careful not to over mash! Place in bowl and set aside.

SEA BASS   Preheat oven to 400°. Take four 8-ounce Sea Bass fillets. Place them on a sheet pan. Cover the top of the fish with 2 tablespoons Seasoning Mix #2. Then dab a "sliver" of butter on top of each fillet. Take ¼ cup water and pour into sheet pan. Place pan in oven and bake for 15-20 minutes.

SAUTÉ PLANTAINS   Heat the (clean) 8" skillet. Add 2 tablespoons butter, ½ tablespoon fresh chopped garlic, ½ tablespoon Seasoning Mix #1, 3 tablespoons olive oil and 6-8 shrimp (cleaned, peeled, de-veined). Sauté for 1 minute. Stir in ¼ cup chicken stock. Then, add plantains. Stir for 2-3 minutes until plantains get soft and glossy.

SERVE   Remove fish from oven. Ladle one cup of avocado puree onto each dinner plate, then place Sea Bass fillet in the middle, top with 2 shrimp. Finish with plantains surrounding. *Serves 4.*

EQUIPMENT LIST

measuring cups and spoons
chopping knife
food processor
2-quart bowl
8" frying pan
potato masher
sheet pan

INGREDIENTS

3 medium-sized, ripe avocados
2 cups medium diced ripe tomatoes
1½ tablespoon fresh chopped garlic
2½ tablespoons Seasoning Mix #1
4 tablespoons Worcestershire sauce
1 medium diced jalapeño (1 tablespoon)
3 tablespoons fresh cut cilantro
¼ cup finely diced onions
¼ cup finely diced red bell pepper
juice from 1 lemon
juice from 1 lime
1 teaspoon salt
¼ cup cold chicken stock
2 green plantains
2 cups corn oil
four 8-ounce Sea Bass fillets
2 tablespoons Seasoning Mix #2
4 "slivers" of butter
2 tablespoons butter
3 tablespoons olive oil
6-8 shrimp (cleaned, peeled, de-veined)
¼ cup chicken stock

CHILEAN SEA BASS WITH AVOCADO PURÉE AND SAUTÉED PLANTAINS

STUFFED FLOUNDER WITH CORN BREAD DRESSING AND CRAWFISH BUTTERCREAM SAUCE

EQUIPMENT LIST

measuring cups and spoons, rubber spatula

chopping knife

3 large mixing bowls

12" x 9¼" x 2½" baking pan

1-quart saucepan, 4-quart saucepan

sifter

two 10" skillets (at least 2" deep)

whip

INGREDIENTS

½ cup cornmeal

2 cups corn flour, 3 cups regular flour

2 tablespoons baking powder

1 teaspoon salt

1½ cups sugar

7 eggs

2½ cups milk

½ pound + 3 tablespoons margarine

3 cups medium diced onion

2 cups medium diced green bell pepper

1 cup medium diced celery

1 tablespoon chopped garlic

½ pan of corn bread (see corn bread recipe)

3½ tablespoons Seasoning Mix #2

5 tablespoons unsalted butter

4 flounders (1½ lbs. each, before de-boning)

1 cup corn oil

1½ cups heavy cream

¼ cup finely diced scallions

½ lb. crawfish tail meat

½ cup finely diced scallions

1 teaspoon corn starch

2 teaspoons warm water

This is one recipe where a jacket is required. It's challenging, but worth the trouble. And the corn bread . . . an absolutely rockin' version of the southern classic.

TO PREPARE

CORN BREAD   Take 2 bowls. To bowl #1, add ½ cup cornmeal, 2 cups corn flour, 2 cups regular flour, 2 tablespoons baking powder, 1 teaspoon salt and 1½ cups sugar. Take sifter and sift ingredients from bowl #1 into empty bowl #2. Take empty bowl #1, add 4 eggs, 2 cups milk and whip together. Heat a 1-quart saucepan and melt ½ pound margarine. Then, combine wet and dry ingredients into bowl #2 and mix thoroughly using a rubber spatula.

Take a baking pan, scoop in 2 tablespoons butter, and place in pre-heated oven (350°). Allow butter to melt completely, then remove pan from oven. Use a paper towel to cover pan, including sides with melted butter. Next, take corn bread mixture, and pour it into the pan. (Tap pan several times on counter so mixture becomes flat and even.) Place pan in oven for approximately 40 minutes. (Test after 30 minutes by running a knife into mixture — when knife comes out clean, corn bread is done.) Let cool. (Note: ½ pan will be used for recipe: the rest is for tomorrow's breakfast *or to serve in baskets on the side!*)

STUFFING   Heat a 10" skillet on high. Add 3 tablespoons margarine and melt. Add 3 cups medium diced onion, 2 cups medium diced green bell pepper, 1 cup medium diced celery and 1 tablespoon chopped garlic.

While veggies are cooking, take one half pan of corn bread and crumble it onto a sheet pan. Place the pan into a pre-heated oven (350°), to toast and dry out the corn bread (approximately 20 minutes).

Check veggies, then stir in 2 tablespoons Seasoning Mix #2 *(see page 32)*. Lower the flame by half, to medium heat. (Cook mixture for approximately 30 minutes.) Check the veggies every two minutes or so, repeating a "stick and scrape" (let the mixture cook, stick, then scrape the bottom and stir back into the mixture as you go). The goal: to caramelize and keep them a little crunchy.

Continued on page 108

STUFFED FLOUNDER WITH CORN BREAD DRESSING AND CRAWFISH BUTTERCREAM SAUCE

(continued)

FLOUNDER Go to your local fish market and ask for 4 whole flounders, cut like jackets. (They should be completely boned-out and slit from the belly, opening up like a jacket. Tail is intact.) At home, cut out back spine, still leaving the tail intact. Then remove gristle from the remaining meat on the sides of the jacket. Also cut out the little strip of bones at top of each flounder on both sides. On each flounder, there should be two flaps, or sides of a jacket, which are separate but still attached at the tail.

BREADING THE FLOUNDER Place 1 cup flour on a plate. Mix in ½ tablespoon Seasoning Mix #2. Take a large bowl, add 3 eggs and ½ cup milk. Whip them together. Dredge both sides of each flounder in the flour mixture, dip in egg wash, then back to the flour. Set to the side.

PAN FRYING THE FLOUNDER Heat 1 cup corn oil in a 10" skillet on a medium flame. Take the breaded flounder fillets, two at a time, side by side and brown them off to a nice, golden brown. When done, place them on a plate covered with paper towels. Place more paper towels over two fillets and repeat.

BACK TO VEGGIES Take half pan of toasted corn bread and crumble into veggie mixture. Mix together. Add ¼ cup heavy cream and 3 tablespoons unsalted butter. Slowly work into mixture, stirring for about five minutes. Last, stir in ½ cup finely diced scallions. Stuffing is done! Spoon stuffing out onto a plate. Place in refrigerator for 15 minutes.

STUFF THE FLOUNDER Take a handful of stuffing and roll it between your hands so it becomes a cylinder shape (about 1" thick). Tuck it in between the jacket flaps of the fillets. Repeat for each fillet.

Place in baking pan and place in preheated oven (350°) for 15 minutes. When finished, place on individual plates or on a platter. (Sauce will be poured over top before serving.)

SAUCE Heat a 4-quart saucepan on a medium flame. Melt 1 tablespoon butter. When melted, add ½ lb. crawfish tail meat, 1 tablespoon Seasoning Mix #2 and cook for 2 minutes. Then add 1½ cups heavy cream and bring mixture to a boil. Stir, reduce flame by half, then let simmer for 3 minutes. (*Note: Keep an eye on pot, cream has a tendency to boil over!*) Next, add another tablespoon butter and ¼ cup finely diced scallions.

Take 1 teaspoon corn starch and 2 teaspoons warm water. Mix together in a coffee cup. Add to sauce and stir for one minute. Pour sauce over fish and serve warm! *Serves* 4.

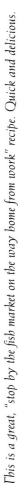

CEDAR ROASTED SALMON WITH FRESH ROSEMARY AND APPLESAUCE

This is a great, "stop by the fish market on the way home from work" recipe. Quick and delicious.

Just one note: pick up the cedar planks ahead of time. And have someone cut them for you. It's hard to saw cedar planks and stir the sauce at the same time.

Special thanks to Nola's restaurant for the inspiration for this dish.

TO PREPARE

SALMON   Preheat oven to 475°. Take 4 salmon fillets (6-8 ounces each), and place each one on a cedar plank. Place the planks on a sheet pan. Take 1 tablespoon Seasoning Mix #1 *(see page 32)* and sprinkle it evenly across the top of salmon fillets. Then, scoop 1 teaspoon butter on top of each fillet. Place them in the oven for about 13 minutes.

PREP APPLES   (Prepare while salmon is cooking.) Take 2 apples and place them core side up (at the top), on a cutting board. Cut both apples into thin slices by cutting the knife downwards, then working all the way around the apple in a circular motion. Cut as much as possible without cutting into the core. *(Note: prepare apples just prior to using them, otherwise they turn brown.)*

SAUCE   Heat a 2-quart sauce pan on a medium flame. Add 1 tablespoon butter. Melt completely. Add 1 tablespoon freshly chopped rosemary, 1 tablespoon freshly chopped garlic and sauté together for about 1 minute. Garlic will become translucent and whitish. (The idea is not to brown the garlic. Keep sauce on a medium flame.) Add 1 tablespoon Seasoning Mix #2 *(see page 32)*, 2 tablespoons Worcestershire sauce, the juice of 1 lemon and 2 cups chicken stock.

Next, raise the flame to high. Bring sauce to a boil. Check salmon fillets. (Remove from oven after 13 minutes.) When sauce reaches a boil, take a spoon and stir in apples and 2 tablespoons butter. *(Note: The apples should be "flexible," a little bit soft, but still a little bit crunchy.)*

Take a pair of tongs, remove the apples from the sauce and place over salmon fillets. Pour sauce, which will be relatively thin, over top and serve warm. *Serves 4.*

EQUIPMENT LIST

measuring cups and spoons
chopping knife
4 cedar planks (12" x 5½", ½" thick)
(Note: Each side should be sanded and washed. Then oiled before each use.)
sheet pan
2-quart sauce pan
spoon
coffee cup
pair of tongs

INGREDIENTS

4 salmon fillets (6-8 ounces each)
1 tablespoon Seasoning Mix #1
4 teaspoons + 3 tablespoons butter
2 apples (sliced very thin)
1 tablespoon freshly chopped rosemary
1 tablespoon freshly chopped garlic
1½ tablespoon Seasoning Mix #2
2 tablespoons Worcestershire sauce
juice of 1 lemon
2 cups chicken stock
2 tablespoons warm water
1 tablespoon corn starch

SHRIMP SMOTHERED IN OKRA AND TOMATO

EQUIPMENT LIST

measuring cups and spoons
chopping knife
spoon
6–8-quart pot
bowl

INGREDIENTS

3 tablespoons margarine
3 cups medium diced onions
1 cup medium diced green bell pepper
1 cup medium diced yellow bell pepper
1 cup medium diced celery
2 tablespoons chopped garlic
3½ tablespoons Seasoning Mix #2
5 cups fresh cut okra (½ inch pieces)
2 cups medium diced plum tomatoes
1 cup chicken stock
24 peeled, butterflied shrimp (16-20 count)
short grain rice (½ cup per person, uncooked)

This dish is inspired by a Creole dish Greg ate one night at The Praline Connection, a restaurant in New Orleans. "I loved it," he said. "It had shrimp, tomatoes and okra. I never tasted anything like it." So here is Greg's recipe, culled from a mouth-watering memory.

TO PREPARE

VEGGIES Heat a 6–8-quart pot. Add 3 tablespoons margarine. When it begins to melt, stir in 3 cups onions, 1 cup green bell pepper, 1 cup yellow bell pepper and 1 cup celery. (All veggies medium diced.) Smother them together. At the 5-minute mark add 2 tablespoons chopped garlic and 2 tablespoons Seasoning Mix #2 (*see page 32*). Continue to sauté, for about 15 minutes total, repeating a "stick and scrape" (let it cook, stick, then scrape the bottom and stir back into vegetable mixture). *Note: The volume of the vegetables will be reduced by half.*

Add 5 cups fresh cut okra (½ inch pieces) into pot. Smother the okra down into the mixture and squeeze out all the sticky, yummy goo. Continue cooking for 10 minutes on medium heat. Then add 2 cups medium diced plum tomatoes and 1 cup chicken stock. Stir occasionally. (There will be plenty of moisture, so no need to worry about stick and scrape anymore.)

SHRIMP Next, take 24 peeled, de-veined and butterflied shrimp. (To butterfly shrimp: take a knife, and run it down the back of the shrimp to open it up. Remove any veins.) Place shrimp in a bowl, stir in ½ tablespoon Seasoning Mix #2 and mix thoroughly. Then, stir shrimp into okra mixture and add another ½ tablespoon Seasoning Mix #2. Cook the shrimp in the sauce approximately 5 minutes.

Serve over white or brown rice. *Serves 4*

SEARED TUNA WITH SMOKIN' RED PEPPER SAUCE AND SAUTÉED SPINACH

A more elegant twist on blackened tuna with sauce to die for. This recipe is for tuna with the great flavor of blackening without all the smoke.

TO PREPARE

PRE-SEASON TUNA   Take two 8-ounce pieces of Yellowfin tuna and season by rubbing 1 tablespoon Seasoning Mix #2 *(see page 32)* evenly over both sides of each piece. Place tuna on a plate and put in refrigerator for one hour.

ROAST PEPPERS   *(Note: 2 large peppers are needed for 2 cups chopped.)* Roasted peppers may be purchased ahead of time or prepared as follows: Using tongs, place one pepper at a time directly over a flame and turn it when side facing flame turns black. Keep turning until entire pepper is black, then place it in a bowl. Cover with plastic wrap, allowing peppers to steam inside bowl for 15-20 minutes. Remove peppers from bowl and rinse off black part. Also, remove seeds and core. Then chop and set aside.

SAUCE   Heat a 2-quart saucepan on a high flame. Add 2 tablespoons olive oil. When oil begins to smoke, add 1 cup medium diced onions and 1 tablespoon fresh chopped garlic. Using a wooden spatula, sauté until light brown (approximately 10 minutes). Keep stirring occasionally, scraping bottom of pan when onions begin to stick. Reduce flame to medium.

Add 2 cups roasted red peppers and 1 tablespoon Seasoning Mix #2. Stir for 2 minutes. Then pour in 1 cup chicken stock. Cook for an additional 7 minutes. Remove from flame. Spoon mixture into a food processor to blend (or spoon mixture into a bowl and use a hand-held mixer). Grind for 30 seconds or until smooth. Pour mixture back into the pot. Return pot to stove.

Add 2 tablespoons heavy cream (or half and half) and return to a simmer. Remove from heat. Sauce is ready. Keep it in a warm place. *(Note: When ready to serve, pour the sauce, which must be cooled to room temperature, into an empty ketchup bottle, then squeeze it out onto the plate in a squiggle . . . presentation is everything.)*

COOKING TUNA   Heat another 2-quart saucepan on low heat. Add 2 tablespoons butter and melt it very slowly.

Continued on page 116

EQUIPMENT LIST

measuring cups and spoons
chopping knife
cutting board
small skillet or wok
large spoon
two 2-quart saucepans
wooden spatula
food processor or a hand-held mixer
bowl
fork
8-10" non-stick skillet
ladle (optional)
plate
tongs
empty plastic ketchup bottle

INGREDIENTS

two 8-ounce pieces of Yellowfin tuna
2 tablespoons Seasoning Mix #2
2 cups roasted red peppers
4 tablespoons olive oil
1 cup medium diced onions
1 tablespoon fresh chopped garlic
1½ cups chicken stock
2 tablespoons heavy cream (or half and half)
2 tablespoons butter
½ tablespoon fresh garlic
1 teaspoon Seasoning Mix #1
5 cups fresh picked spinach

SEARED TUNA WITH SMOKIN' RED PEPPER SAUCE AND SAUTÉED SPINACH

(continued)

Place an 8-10" non-stick skillet on another burner and turn on medium heat. Remove tuna from the refrigerator and scoop melted butter on top of each piece. Place tuna in skillet and cook approximately 2 minutes on each side, for medium rare. Remove and place on cutting board. Cut tuna into ½" strips.

Prepare spinach: In small skillet or wok, heat 2 tablespoons olive oil and add ½ tablespoon fresh garlic, 1 teaspoon Seasoning Mix #1 (*see page* 32) and quickly sauté 5 cups fresh picked spinach. Add ½ cup chicken stock and sauté until spinach is warm (approximately 1 minute). Pull from heat.

Take dinner plates, ladle sauce (or squiggle if using plastic ketchup bottle) onto plates first, then layer tuna strips on top. Mold a large spoonful of spinach in middle of plate. *Serves 2*

BANANAS FOSTER

EQUIPMENT LIST

8-10" skillet

INGREDIENTS

1 cup dark brown sugar
½ pound butter
¼ cup triple sec liqueur
4 large ripe sliced bananas

Sultry, hot and soothing. Sweet. Like the Big Easy.

TO PREPARE

Heat a 8-10" skillet on a medium flame. Add 1 cup dark brown sugar, ½ pound butter and ¼ cup triple sec liqueur. Mix together and cook until melted. Add 4 large ripe sliced bananas. Lower flame, and let simmer for approximately 10 minutes. Pour mixture into a bowl. Serve with vanilla ice cream.

SERVING SUGGESTION   Pour into one large bowl, pass out 4 spoons and share.

FOR THE ADVENTUROUS   After pouring mixture into bowl, add 1 ounce 151 liquor and light it with a match. When the flame goes out, stir in ½ cup toasted, sliced almonds. *Serves 4.*

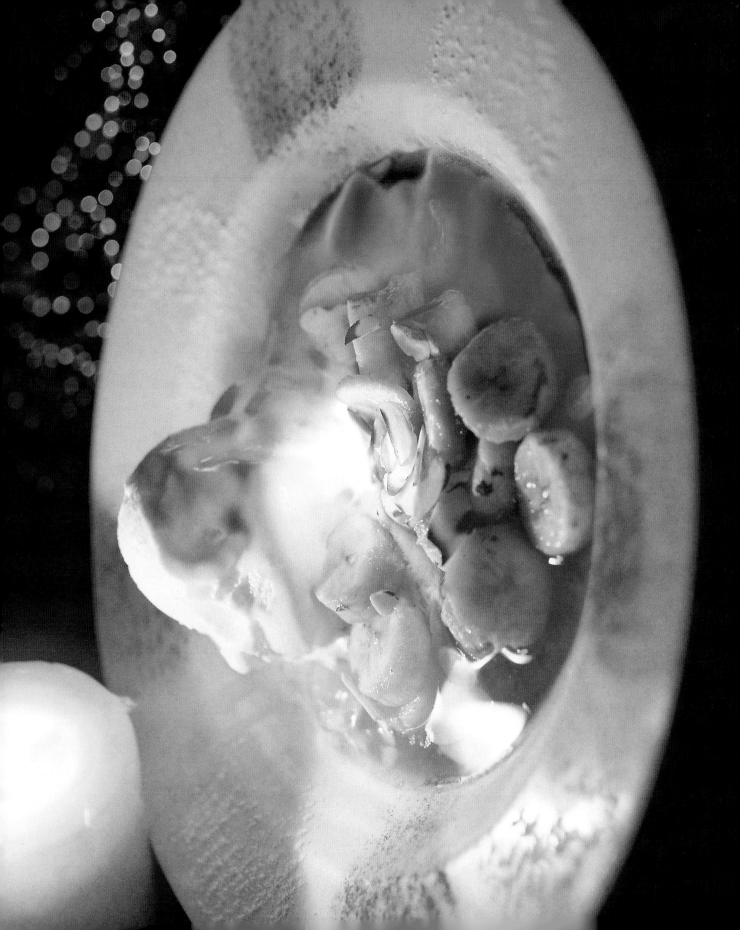

DOUBLE CHOCOLATE PILE ON THE POUNDS CAKE WITH STRAWBERRY SAUCE

As Greg says, "Oh Lordy..."

TO PREPARE

WET MIX   Preheat oven to 325°. Take mixing bowl and add ½ pound butter (sweet, unsalted). Slowly stir in 1⅔ cups sugar, a bit at a time. Add 5 eggs, one at a time, folding in with a large spoon. Next, stir in 1 teaspoon vanilla extract.

DRY MIX   In another bowl, add dry mix of: 1½ cups cake flour, ½ cup cocoa powder, ½ teaspoon salt and ⅛ teaspoon white pepper. Sift together. Take dry mix and 1 cup chocolate chips and fold into butter/sugar mixture. Be careful not to over mix.

GREASE PAN   Take a 9" x 5" pan. Grease the pan with butter. Then coat butter with thin layer of flour (¼ cup). Shake pan, distributing flour evenly. Discard the extra flour (the little bit that doesn't stick to the butter).

POUR AND BAKE   Pour mixture into the pan. Bake for one hour. (*Or, do the toothpick test: stick in toothpick, pull it out. If it come comes out clean . . . done!*) Remove from oven. Let cool 1 hour at room temperature.

STRAWBERRY SAUCE   Take 2 pints fresh strawberries. Cut off the tops, slice into quarters and place them in a colander. Wash pieces, then place them in a bowl. Add 2 tablespoons sugar, 2 teaspoons vanilla and mix together. Take ¼ of strawberry mixture, scoop into food processor, and grind until smooth. Pour back into bowl of strawberry mixture. Place bowl in refrigerator.

WHIPPED CREAM   Take 2 cups heavy whipping cream, ¼ cup sugar, 1 tablespoon vanilla and 1 teaspoon cinnamon. Whip together for whipped cream with a fluffy, meringue-textured consistency. (*Note: do not over whip.*) Place in bowl and set in refrigerator.

SERVE   Remove strawberry sauce and whipped cream from refrigerator. Cut poundcake into squares and layer with strawberry sauce and whipped cream (make 3 layers). Top with a little whipped cream, vanilla ice cream and several fresh strawberry pieces. Finish with a pinch of powdered sugar in a sifter and sprinkle top of dessert. *Serves 2-4*

EQUIPMENT LIST

measuring cups and spoons
chopping knife
cutting board
large spoon
2 mixing bowls
9" x 5" pan
toothpick
colander
whip
sifter

INGREDIENTS

½ pound butter (sweet unsalted)
1⅔ cups sugar
5 eggs
1 teaspoon vanilla extract
1½ cups cake flour
½ cup cocoa powder
½ teaspoon salt
⅛ teaspoon white pepper
1 cup chocolate chips   (use small chips)
2 pints fresh strawberries

CHOCOLATE, CHOCOLATE CRÈME BRULEE

EQUIPMENT LIST

measuring cups and spoons
cutting board
chopping knife
whisk
mixing bowl
roasting pan (9" x 12")
roasting pan (10" x 13" or larger)
aluminum foil
3" round cookie cutter
electric mixer
sheet pan
parchment paper
1-quart saucepan
saucepan for double boiler

INGREDIENTS

8 egg yolks
7 eggs
1½ liters milk
8 ounces cold sweet butter
1½ cups + 12 ounces sugar
1½ cups flour
⅛ teaspoon + pinch of salt
½ cup cocoa powder
8 ounces Lindt Excellence (or another premium brand) chocolate bar
4 ounces heavy cream
4 ounces unsweetened chocolate
1 tablespoon butter
1 cup light cream
½ teaspoon vanilla extract

TO PREPARE

CRÈME BRULEE Preheat oven to 350°. Add 8 egg yolks, 7 whole eggs and 12 ounces sugar into a mixing bowl. Whisk together vigorously, then add milk and combine all ingredients. Pour mixture into a roasting pan (9" x 12") and cover with aluminum foil (shiny side down).

Fill a larger roasting pan (10" x 13" or larger) halfway with hot water and submerge smaller (covered) roasting pan into this. Place both pans in oven and bake until mixture is set in the middle (approximately 25-35 minutes). Remove from oven. Let cool.

Place in freezer. When frozen, pop mixture out of pan onto cutting board. Using a 3" round cookie cutter, cut out 8 circles. Place on a pan (lined with parchment paper). Cover with aluminum foil and refrigerate.

CHOCOLATE SHORT BREAD Combine 8 ounces cold sweet butter and ½ cup sugar in mixing bowl. Take an electric mixer and beat with the paddle attachment for 20 seconds on medium speed. Add 1½ cups flour, a pinch of salt, and ½ cup cocoa powder and continue mixing on medium speed.

When dough comes together, transfer to a lightly floured board and roll out to ¼" thick. Take a 3" cookie cutter and cut out 8 circles. Transfer to parchment paper lined sheet pan. (Place cookie circles so they are not touching.) Freeze for 1 hour.

Preheat oven to 250°. Place pan in oven until cookies are firm (approximately 45 minutes – 1 hour). Remove from oven. Cool and set aside.

CHOCOLATE GANACHE Take 8 ounce Lindt Excellence chocolate bar. Chop into fine pieces and place in a bowl. Heat a 1-quart saucepan on a medium flame. Add 4 ounces heavy cream and bring to a boil. When cream reaches a boil, pour over chocolate. Whisk ingredients together until homogenous. Let cool at room temperature until thick.

Continued on page 124

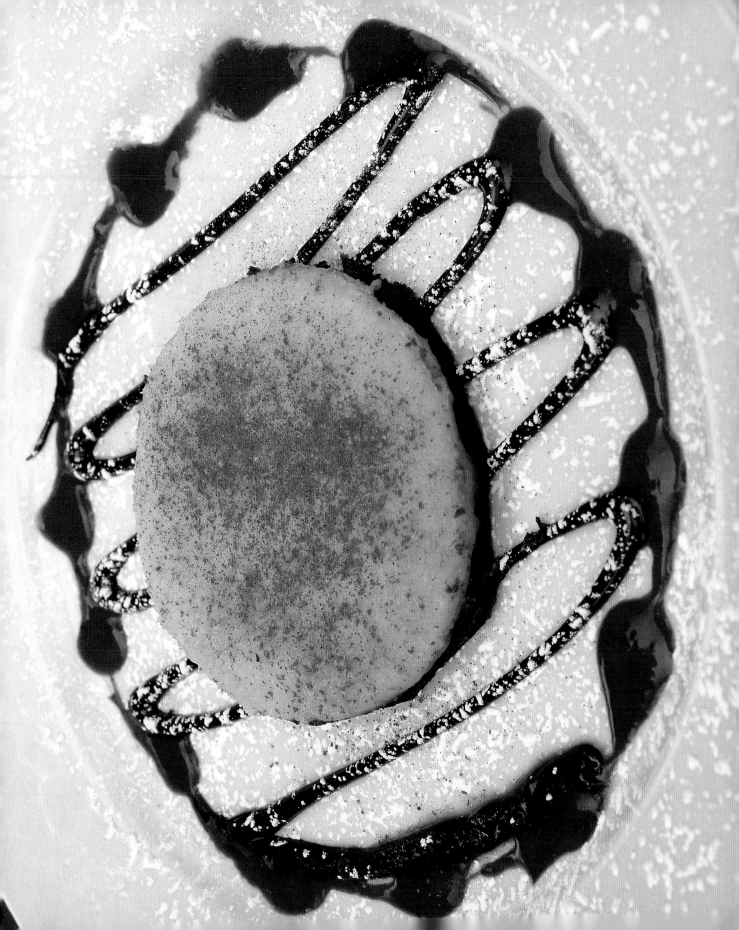

CHOCOLATE, CHOCOLATE CRÈME BRULEE

(continued)

CHOCOLATE SAUCE

Take a saucepan, add a small amount of water (approximately 1 inch) and bring it to a boil. Then set up a double boiler by placing a bowl on top of the pan. (The bowl should fit snugly on top). Add 4 ounces unsweetened chocolate to bowl and melt. Slowly, add 1 cup sugar, $\frac{1}{8}$ teaspoon salt, and 1 tablespoon butter. Then, gradually stir in 1 cup light cream. Stir until smooth.

Remove bowl from double boiler and place onto direct heat until sauce thickens. Remove from heat and stir in $\frac{1}{2}$ teaspoon vanilla extract. Set aside at room temperature.

ASSEMBLY OF DESSERT

Set oven to broil. Remove brulee from refrigerator and sprinkle with granulated sugar. Cook brulee in broiler until the top is caramelized.

Using a spoon, scoop chocolate sauce in the middle of dessert plate. Scoop a large ball of ganache and place it in the middle, over the sauce. Place a shortbread cookie on top and push down gently. Using a spatula, place brulee on top of cookie. Repeat for all cookies.

Serve immediately. *Serves 8.*

STUFFED PEAR WITH SEASONAL BERRIES

If some New Yorker tells you to "stuff it," maybe this is what he means.

TO PREPARE

PREP / COOK PEARS
Preheat oven to 350°. Take 4 ripe Anjou pears. Cut the tops off and set aside. Do not discard! Then, core the pears. With a spoon, remove as much meat as possible from inside pear and place into a bowl. Set aside.

Place 4 pears, including their tops in a roasting pan. Fill pan with water, just enough to cover bottom (approximately ¼"). Cover pan with aluminum foil and place in oven. Blanch pears until soft but not mushy (approximately 15 minutes). Remove pears from oven. Place on a plate and put in refrigerator.

FILLING
Take ½ pint each seasonal berries (combination of raspberries, blueberries and strawberries is great. Total: 1½ pints). Cut and clean strawberries (remove and discard tops, cut into quarters, then wash). Wash raspberries and blueberries. Place all washed fruit in a bowl. Add 2 tablespoons sugar, ½ tablespoon vanilla extract and 2 tablespoons water. Mix thoroughly with a spoon. Scoop ¼ of mixture into food processor and grind it up until smooth. Scoop liquid back into bowl.

Take bowl containing pear meat and stir into bowl containing berries.

SERVE
Remove pears from refrigerator and place on individual plates. Scoop berry mixture into each pear, filling each one. Garnish each plate with a pear top. *Serves 4.*

SERVING SUGGESTION
Serve each pear on a bed of whipped cream or scoop spoonful of berry mixture on plate, add dollop whipped cream on the side, then add pear. (See directions for whipped cream under *Double Chocolate Pile on the Pounds Recipe* found on page 121.)

EQUIPMENT LIST
measuring cups and spoons
chopping knife
paring knife or corer
cutting board
spoon
2 bowls
food processor
plate

INGREDIENTS
4 ripe Anjou pears
1½ pint seasonal berries
2 tablespoons sugar
½ tablespoon vanilla extract
2 tablespoons water